PATHWAYS TO
PEACE
OF MIND

NAPOLEON HILL

Published and Distributed by
SOUND WISDOM
PO Box 310
Shippensburg, PA 17257-0310
717-530-2122
info@soundwisdom.com
www.soundwisdom.com

ISBN 13: 978-1-64095-398-7
ISBN 13 eBook: 978-1-64095-399-4

For Worldwide Distribution, Printed in the U.S.A.
1 2 3 4 5 6 / 26 25 24 23 22

CONTENTS

FOREWORD

Napoleon Hill's grandson, Dr. J. B. Hill, is one of the trustees of the Napoleon Hill Foundation and recently gave the Foundation a manuscript Napoleon had given to his son David, J. B.'s father, in the 1950s. Napoleon had titled it "How to Get Peace of Mind" and had intended to publish it as a series of newspaper columns. For reasons unknown to the Foundation, the writings were never published. They are presented here for the first time.

The trustees have combined this manuscript with a previously unpublished excerpt from an unfinished autobiographical work written by Napoleon in 1947 and with editorial essays written by Napoleon and published in 1919 and 1920 in his magazine, *Hill's Golden Rule*. These writings were selected for this book because they all explore the subject of attaining peace of mind, one of the primary components of a happy life, as envisioned by Napoleon Hill. A final chapter is a previously unpublished transcript of a 1948 radio program in which Napoleon disclosed what single ability is essential to achieving success and happiness.

Readers familiar with Napoleon Hill's bestselling book *Think and Grow Rich* may associate his writings with teachings on how to achieve monetary success, and indeed that was one of the subjects of the book. But Napoleon believed that the greatest success in life was not monetary and that true riches came from the peace of mind one achieves by helping others. In fact, his last book, published in 1967 when he was 84 years old, is titled *Grow Rich with Peace of Mind* and deals exclusively with this subject.

There are numerous writers who have chosen to devote their lives to the study of self-help. Napoleon Hill is one of the most famous self-help authors, but there were other authors who studied this subject before him. Samuel Smiles wrote a book called *Self-Help* in 1859 in order to help others know about the concept of self-improvement. He wrote about individuals who spent many years working hard and overcoming adversity in order to achieve their goals. Napoleon Hill read Samuel Smiles's book and was heavily influenced by it when he began writing his own self-help books in the early 20th century. However, one difference between Napoleon Hill's books and other self-helps books, including Smiles's, is that Napoleon showed readers *how* to be successful. He listed detailed steps to be taken to achieve success, or any other desired accomplishment in life.

It could aptly be said that Napoleon Hill was a "how to" author. *Think and Grow Rich*, his most famous work, provides six steps that can be used to obtain anything one desires in life, though his main focus there was on attaining financial success. The steps are listed below:

- *First*, fix in your mind the exact amount of money you desire. It is not sufficient merely to say, "I want plenty of money." Be definite as to the amount. (There is a psychological reason for definiteness which will be described in a subsequent chapter.)

- *Second*, determine exactly what you intend to give in return for the money you desire. (There is no such reality as "something for nothing.")

- *Third*, establish a definite date when you intend to possess the money you desire.

- *Fourth*, create a definite plan for attaining what you desire, and begin at once, whether you are ready or not, to put this plan into action.

- *Fifth*, write out a clear, concise statement of the amount of money you intend to acquire, name the time limit for its acquisition, state what you intend to give in return for the money, and describe clearly the plan by which you intend to accumulate it.

- *Sixth*, read your written statement aloud, twice daily, once just before retiring at night and once after arising in the morning. As you read, see and feel and believe yourself already in possession of the money.

These steps can be adapted to guide you to anything you desire. In this little book, *Pathways to Peace of Mind*, Napoleon Hill will show you how to use these steps, and other success principles, to achieve the great gift of Peace of Mind.

—Don Green, executive director and CEO,
Napoleon Hill Foundation

PART
ONE

HOW TO GET PEACE OF MIND

INTRODUCTION

by Dr. J. B. Hill

My first memory of my grandfather is from when I was 12 years old. He gave me a copy of *Think and Grow Rich* and a ten-dollar bill. I did not read the book, and I cannot remember what happened to that ten dollars.

My father, Napoleon Hill's son, went into the military as a young man and served in World War II and the Korean War. He made a career serving his country and won many medals for valor and accomplishments in active duty. He is buried at Arlington National Cemetery.

I chose to follow in the footsteps of my father and joined the United States Marine Corps, where I served for 26 years. During this time, I received my degree from Vanderbilt University and finally read my grandfather's book, *Think and Grow Rich*, for the first time. After I retired from the Marines, I decided to attend medical school at age 46 and am still practicing medicine today.

I am extremely proud of my grandfather, for his work has helped millions of individuals achieve their dreams. I serve as a member of the Board of Trustees of the Napoleon Hill Foundation, and through the Foundation we have helped countless people achieve their own level of success.

The first portion of the book you are about to read was given to my father when he returned from the Korean War in 1953. Recently, I was going through my father's collection of material and located the manuscript, titled "How to Get Peace of Mind." According to the cover page, it was meant to be a series of newspaper columns, but it was never published. It is not unusual for my grandfather's writings to be unpublished, because he was so prolific. His works are still being discovered by his family and the Foundation now, more than 50 years after his death.

As a grandson who has a burning desire to perpetuate my grandfather's legacy, I hope you enjoy reading this instructive, inspiring, and timeless gem of a book, which is finally seeing the light, deservedly, after being hidden away for nearly seven decades.

INTRODUCTION

by Napoleon Hill

PEACE OF MIND softens poverty and adorns riches.
−NAPOLEON HILL

Peace of Mind is for sale to all who will pay the price, but not at cheap bargain prices. Through this series of personal messages, you will be told what is peace of mind, its price and how to get it.

Before beginning our search for peace of mind, let us find out precisely what it is for which we are searching. It consists in many circumstances and many things, each of which has a price tag clearly marked and attached to it.

First of all, peace of mind is complete mastery over all forms of worry.

It is freedom from want of the physical necessities of life.

It is freedom from physical and mental ailments, when and where their causes may be removed or transmuted into something desirable.

It is freedom from the fears and superstitions of the past which have held mankind in bondage.

It is freedom from the Seven Basic Fears:

1. Fear of poverty

2. Fear of criticism

3. Fear of ill health

4. Fear of loss of love

5. Fear of loss of liberty

6. Fear of old age

7. Fear of death

It is freedom from the common human weakness of seeking something for nothing—for life on a cheap, bargain-price basis.

It is the habit of doing one's own thinking on all subjects, a prerogative given to man by his Maker which happens to be the only thing over which an individual has the complete power of control at all times.

It is the habit of frequent self-inspection from within to determine what changes one must make in his character.

It is the habit of developing the courage to look at the facts of life as a realist, not as a dreamer.

It is the habit of controlling greed and the desire to be great and powerful and rich at the expense of others.

It is the habit of helping others to help themselves.

It is recognition of the truth that everyone has the privilege of approach to, and the free use of, the power of Infinite Intelligence for the solution of all human problems.

It is freedom from anxiety over what may happen after the transformation known as death.

It is freedom from all desire for revenge.

It is the habit of "Going the Extra Mile" in all human relationships; of rendering more service and better service than one is paid for and doing it in a positive mental attitude.

It is a keen understanding of the difference between the possession of things and the privilege of using things for the benefit of others.

It is knowing who you are and what are your true virtues and abilities which distinguish you from all others.

It is freedom from the habit of transmuting defeat into a state of mind of discouragement.

It is the habit of thinking in terms of that which you desire, not in thinking of the obstacles which may get in your way while you are seeking to attain it.

It is the habit of starting right where you stand, to do that which you wish, instead of waiting for all circumstances to be favorable for your doing it.

It is the habit of laughing at the petty misfortunes which overtake you, recognizing that they may turn out to be blessings instead.

It is the habit of looking for the seed of an equivalent benefit which consists in all adversities, defeats, and failures, instead of mourning over them as a loss. Nothing in human experience is ever entirely lost.

It is the habit of taking life in stride, neither shrinking from the disagreeable nor overindulging in the pleasantries.

It is the habit of getting happiness from doing rather than seeking it in possessing.

It is the habit of making life pay off on your own terms, in values of your own choosing, rather than settling for a menial's hire.

It is the habit of giving before trying to get.

So, you see that Peace of Mind is quite an institution. It can be attained only by the means of a definite formula which will be revealed through this series of personal messages from one who has attained it.

The secret behind this formula came into my possession only after I had devoted almost forty years to the work of analyzing men who had become successes in the accumulation of material riches.

Of all the more than six hundred top-ranking men who revealed to me the secrets of financial success, I found no evidence that any of them had found lasting peace of mind! This realization was so shocking that it left me no choice but that of searching for the way to peace of mind.

And when I found the way, I was surprised to learn that it is within the reach of every human being who is willing to follow the blueprint which I shall reveal through these personal messages.

There is a Master Key which opens all doors between one and peace of mind. It will not be revealed until we reach the last of these personal messages because the initiate must first learn how to use the key, through the assimilation of these messages.

You have not found success unless you are
at peace with yourself and all others.
−NAPOLEON HILL

CHAPTER 1

THE ART OF SHARING RICHES

Success in its highest and noblest form calls for
peace of mind and enjoyment and happiness, which comes
only to the man who has found the work he likes best.
—NAPOLEON HILL

"When you are worried by a problem you cannot solve," said John Wanamaker, department store tycoon and philanthropist, "and do not know what to do next, there is always one thing you can do which may either solve your problem or lead eventually to its solution: You can look around until you find someone with a greater problem than yours and start right where you stand to help him finds its solution. The chances are a thousand to one that by the time the solution to the other fellow's problem has been found, you will have also found the solution to your own."

From the day when I first heard this strange philosophy, I began to observe more closely those who have problems, including myself, and found the advice to be sound.

Andrew Carnegie understood the soundness of this philosophy—the habit of helping others in order to help one's self—and that is why he commissioned me to take to the people of the world what he called the better portion of his vast riches, which consisted of the "know-how" through which he accumulated his fortune.

Mr. Carnegie was a master in the art of sharing his riches, having done such a fine job of sharing opportunities with his employees and business associates that he has been credited with having made more millionaires than has any other American industrialist. He discovered that it paid to share one's blessings—paid in two ways: first, in the peace of mind one experiences when he helps another to attain success; secondly, in material riches.

Willingness to share one's blessings is one of the twelve great riches of life. It ranks, in importance, very near to a positive mental attitude, which is the first and most important of the twelve great riches. Now let us see how this principle works out in practice.

During World War II, one of my distinguished students, Mr. Edward Choate, of Los Angeles, California, a representative of the New England Mutual Life Insurance Company, so budgeted his time that 80 percent of it was given to the government in helping to sell war bonds, for which he received no direct compensation. Ten percent of his time was devoted to counseling and training other life insurance men—his competitors—in the successful selling of life insurance, for which he neither asked nor received compensation. The remaining 10 percent of his time was devoted to his own business of selling life insurance.

One might think that a budget which gave away 90 percent of a man's time would be ruinous. Well, let us take a look at the record. During the first three months of one year, Mr. Choate wrote more than $3,000,000 in life insurance, most of it having been written in his own office, on the lives of men who came voluntarily and made application for insurance, men whom he had contacted in connection with the service he rendered while giving away 90 percent of his time. This is more life insurance than the average agent sells during ten years of hard work.

Every time you share your blessings with another, you place someone in your debt and become his creditor. It is better to be a creditor than it is to be a debtor, for debts have to be paid off.

Edward Choate was first introduced to the principle of sharing one's blessings through one of my books on the philosophy of personal achievement. Every year, he autographs and gives away hundreds of copies of this book, and every book attracts to him new friends who often remember him when they are in the market for life insurance. It is little wonder, therefore, that most of his life insurance business is done in his own office.

Mr. Choate's habit of giving away autographed copies of this particular success book is by no means motivated entirely by his desire to write life insurance on the lives of those to whom he presents it, for he often gives the book to men and women who, by no stretch of the imagination, ever will become buyers of life insurance. He gives the book away because he found himself through its philosophy at a crucial period of his life, when he needed some sources of outside inspiration. He gives it as an expression of his gratitude for the help it gave him.

Edward Choate is one of those rare individuals who have learned that one cannot remain forever on the receiving side of life and expect to get or to keep peace of mind or financial prosperity. He has learned, along with the great philosophers of all times, that only the riches one gives away may one keep. If I can get this truth across so that it takes a firm hold on your imagination, the reading of this personal message may well mark the most important turning point of your life, no matter who you are or how rich you may now be.

For more than forty years I have been on the sharing end of life, having been commissioned by Andrew Carnegie to organize a success philosophy through which he desired to share with the people of this world his fabulous billion-dollar fortune, as well as the "know-how" with which he acquired his tangible riches. So, I am not without personal knowledge of the benefits available to one through the principle of sharing.

The habit of sharing one's blessings not only leads to peace of mind, but it places one in a favorable position to benefit by the great Law of Compensation described by Ralph Waldo Emerson, for it is true that whatsoever a man does to or for another he does to or for himself.

Application of this principle of sharing of blessings would bring harmony out of chaos in the unfortunate relationship existing between management and industrial workers if both sides adopted it and lived by it in good faith. I introduced the principle in the industrial plant of the R. G. LeTourneau Company, located in Toccoa, Georgia, with such telling results that the production costs were reduced far below the costs in the three additional plants of this company. Moreover, personal gripes on the part of employees were entirely eliminated.

You desire peace of mind? Very well, start right where you stand and begin helping those nearest you to find it. Your help may consist of only a few words of encouragement at the proper moment, or it may be something more tangible, but whatever its scope may be, you will feel instantaneous reaction to your efforts in the form of greater peace of mind.

> If you wish to be favorably recognized by others,
> try casting yourself as the part of the good
> Samaritan as often as possible.
> —NAPOLEON HILL

CHAPTER 2

LEARN TO LIVE YOUR OWN LIFE

*The most practiced of all methods for controlling
the mind is the habit of keeping it busy with
a definite purpose, backed by a definite plan.*
—NAPOLEON HILL

The most profound truth known to mankind consists in the fact that the Creator provided man with the complete, unchallengeable right to control his own mind; to direct it to whatever ends he may desire, good or bad, success or failure.

The privilege of exercising this prerogative over the mind is the only thing over which man has complete control. By the simple process of exercising this privilege, one may lift himself to great heights of achievement in any field or endeavor. The exercise of this right represents the major difference between men who succeed in life and those who drift into failure; and it is a "must" for the man who seeks peace of mind. There can be no peace for the mind which is not under its owner's complete control at all times.

A controlled mind may achieve great success in any chosen field of endeavor without the aid of a formal education. For proof of this fact observe the achievements of Thomas A. Edison, who became the world's greatest inventor by guiding the work of formally educated men with his own controlled mind.

Henry Ford became America's greatest industrialist and made himself richer than he needed to be, not because of his superior ability or brains, but simply by taking possession of his own mind and directing it to a definite purpose of his own choice. He kept his mind so filled with definiteness of purpose that it had no time left to think about failure and defeat and discouragement. Mr. Ford had but little formal education and he chose a definite major purpose for his lifework which met with ridicule and antagonism from an unfriendly world.

The wealth created and the millions of jobs provided by the two self-controlled minds of Henry Ford and Thomas A. Edison stagger the imagination of the keenest minds, and perhaps changed the entire course of civilization to a more orderly and efficient direction.

Did Edison and Ford find peace of mind? No one could answer this except the two men themselves, but it is known that they attained about everything else they desired, that they recognized no such reality as the "impossible," and it is safe to conjecture that if they did not find peace of mind, they did not seek it.

Orville and Wilbur Wright learned how to live their own lives. Their exercise of this prerogative gave the world its first successful flying machine, a forerunner of a method of transportation which has so shortened the distance between all points on earth that all people have become more closely akin, and may eventually learn how to live together peacefully.

Like Ford and Edison, the Wright Brothers also directed their efforts toward the attainment of a definite purpose which met with ridicule from an unbelieving world. It is worthy of note that the man who takes full possession of his own mind always has great capacity for belief, while the man who allows his mind to drift without aim or purpose invariably is a great unbeliever.

More than forty years ago, Andrew Carnegie sold me an idea which, to date, has brought riches in many forms to many millions of people throughout two-thirds of the civilized world. He sold me the idea that I could take possession of my own mind and direct it to the organization of a philosophy of personal achievement which would give to the man of the streets the full benefit of the "know-how" of success as it had been learned by the trial-and-error method of such men as Mr. Carnegie. I was so unprepared for such a colossal assignment that I barely knew the definition of the word "philosophy," but I did have one asset of priceless value—the capacity for belief. Through the application of that capacity, I induced more than six hundred of the top-ranking successes in America to collaborate with me in presenting the world with its first practical philosophy of individual achievement. Moreover, I stopped the world from pushing me around while I was doing the job, although I met with severe ridicule at first, much of it from my closest relatives, who believed I should give up my fantastic idea and go to work!

I stood by my guns through twenty years of unremunerative research, at the end of which I opened a sealed message left to me by Andrew Carnegie and discovered from its contents that I had been given the assignment to produce a philosophy of individual achievement, selected in competition with more than two hundred others, solely because of my inherent capacity to take possession of my own mind and direct it to a given end despite opposition. My lack of formal education was not considered a handicap.

This personal experience is here related in order that you may know how I came by my belief in the power of the habit of one's learning how to take possession of his own mind.

When Madam Schumann-Heink was a very young girl, she aspired to become a singer. She was sent by her parents to a very noted music teacher for a test of her voice, after which the teacher said, "Go back to your work as a seamstress. You may learn to sew; you will never learn to sing." That advice was perhaps the greatest blessing Schumann-Heink ever experienced. It inspired her with the determination to take possession of her own mind and do with it what she desired. In one easy lesson, she learned how to live her own life and lived to discover that the lesson paid off handsomely in terms she desired most. She became a highly acclaimed operatic diva.

Helen Keller has served well to teach us the value of control of the mind. Despite the loss of the two most important of the five senses, seeing and hearing, Miss Keller took possession of her diminished capabilities and demonstrated to the entire world that our only limitations in the use of mind power are those which we set up for ourselves, or permit others to set up for us.

DEFINITENESS OF PURPOSE

Definiteness of Purpose is the beginning of all human achievements worthy of mention. It is also an indispensable factor in the attainment of peace of mind, for it is an established fact that peace of mind is something one must go after with both plan and purpose, backed by the determination to get it.

During the latter part of the first administration of President Franklin D. Roosevelt, he sent for Henry Ford to visit him at the White House. The invitation caused much excitement among newspapermen, due to the fact that General Hugh Johnson, then the head of the ill-fated National Recovery Administration or NRA, had threatened to "crack down" on Henry Ford for noncompliance with the NRA regulations. When Ford emerged from his visit at the White House, he was pounced upon by newspapermen who wanted to know what he and the president talked about and the reason for his visit.

In his usual succinct way, Ford said, "To tell you the truth, gentlemen, I came to Washington to let the president of the United States see a man who did not come after anything and who wanted no favors from him." The interview was over, but there probably was not a man among these newspapermen who did not envy Mr. Ford because of the evidence he had presented that he had found peace of mind. A rich, recognized, successful man without worries, which destroy peace of mind, was a rare find then, when the entire nation was in the throes of its worst business depression. The president may have been worried, but Henry Ford was not.

Careful analysis of the Ford business record, over a period of more than a quarter of a century, disclosed that his most noteworthy trait, the one which aided him in succeeding more than all other traits, was his great capacity to fix his mind on what he wanted and keep it free from everything he did not want.

My twenty years of research into the causes of success disclosed thirty-one major causes of failure, the first and most frequent of which was the habit of fixing the mind upon the circumstances and things one does not want, such as fear, anxiety, envy, greed, defeat, and failure. There can be no peace of mind where these or similar negative states of mind prevail.

Once when I asked Henry Ford how he managed to keep his mind positive at all times, he replied, "I keep it so busy thinking about the things I wish to do that it has no time for the things I do not wish to do." And here you have a fine formula for conditioning the mind for attainment of peace.

"And where," I asked Mr. Ford, "did you get the foundation for that sound philosophy?"

"I got it," he replied, "from recognition that keeping my mind fixed on the things I wished to do always brought the ways and means of doing them, while thinking about obstacles which might get in my way just as definitely brought defeat."

The Ford success can be described in one sentence: he set his mind to the task of building the world's most dependable automobile at the lowest possible cost to the owners and never stopped until he saw his definite purpose fulfilled.

The automotive graveyard is literally filled with would-be competitors of Ford, nearly all of whom started with more education, more capital, and more "know-how" in the automotive field than he had to begin with, but not one of whom came within sight of catching up with him in practical achievements.

I ran down the records of many of these men and discovered, among other interesting facts, that nearly all of them were trying to imitate Ford instead of endeavoring to excel him. Instead of having a purpose of their own, they were borrowing Ford's purpose and hanging themselves with it. I have seen the same thing happen hundreds of times, in other fields of endeavor, where men failed because they had no definite purpose of their own but tried to borrow that of someone else.

One of the conditions under which Andrew Carnegie commissioned me to organize the philosophy of individual achievement was that I should work without subsidy from him or anyone else, earning my own way as I went. The condition seemed harsh at the time, but subsequent events proved its soundness. Having thus been thrown upon my own resources at the outset, I was forced to begin using the success principles I was gathering for my success philosophy. This led to the immediate application of the first of the seventeen principles of success, Definiteness of Purpose, which I applied to the business of training salesmen, from which I earned enough money to aid me in carrying on my twenty years of research. Also, it led me to the discovery of a sound philosophy of benefit to every person who makes use of it, which can be stated in one sentence:

Every adversity carries with it the seed of an equivalent benefit.

That which seemed to be an adversity, because of the harsh condition Mr. Carnegie had pinned on me, turned out instead to be a great blessing, and it led to one of the seventeen principles of success through which one may transmute all failures and all temporary defeats into factors of success of equivalent power.

Definiteness of Purpose is a great stimulator of the imagination, as Henry Ford demonstrated when he gave instructions to his engineers to draw plans for an engine cylinder block cast in one piece instead of the then-customary two pieces.

"That," said one of the engineers, "is impossible."

"You use that word *impossible* carelessly," Ford exclaimed. "Go ahead and try it." Plan after plan was tested without success. The reason for the failure of the plans, as Ford later said, was the fact that those engineers had sold themselves on that word *impossible* and they were trying hard to live up to it.

Finally, Ford gave the order to the engineering department to "cease work on all other projects until you learn how to cast a cylinder block in one piece." A few hours later, a cylinder block cast in one piece was sent in from the foundry. One man who decided it had to be done made up his mind to experiment with metal in the foundry instead of on paper in the drafting room, and he found the answer.

Henry Ford needed capital—lots of it—to carry on his vast industrial empire. He made up his mind to get it from sources which would not claim the right, in return, to control his business. He came up with a plan through which he got his working capital from the men who would profit most by his operations, the distributors of his automobiles. And the Ford works still are in the hands of the Ford family, thanks to his use of definiteness of purpose.

THE MAGIC POWER OF BELIEF

At the close of World War I, a young soldier who had been in the service came to see me about helping him find a job. At the very outset, he announced, "All I seek is a meal ticket; a place to sleep and enough to eat." The look in his eyes, a sort of glassy stare, told me that hope was dead in his heart. Here was a man willing to settle with life for a mere meal ticket when I knew well enough that if he were made to undergo a change of mental attitude, he could set as his goal a king's ransom and get it.

Something inside me prompted this question: "How would you like to become a multimillionaire? Why settle for a meal ticket when you can settle for millions in cash just as easily?"

"Please don't try to be funny with me," he exclaimed. "I am hungry and need a meal ticket."

"No," I replied. "I am not trying to be funny with you. I am serious, and I can help you make millions if you are willing to use the assets you have and set your goal at the higher figures."

"What do you mean assets?" he queried.

"Why, the assets of a potentially positive mind," I replied. "Now let us take inventory and find out what tangible assets you possess in the way of ability, experience, and the like. We will start there."

By questioning, I discovered that this young soldier had been a door-to-door salesman of brushes before he went to war. Also, that during the war he spent considerable time doing "Kitchen Patrol," or K.P., duty, during which he had learned to cook.

Therefore, his total assets consisted in his ability to cook and his past experience in selling. In the ordinary walks of life, neither cooking nor selling would be likely to lift a man into a multimillionaire class, but this young soldier was taken out of the "ordinary walks" of life by the process of introducing him to his own mind and selling him on its capacity to achieve whatever it could conceive and believe.

During the two hours I had been talking with this young man, my own mind had been at work, analyzing the potentialities of his two assets. Placing these two assets together—the ability to sell and the ability to cook—I quickly assembled them into a plan by which he might convert them into a fortune of sizeable proportions.

"Now, if I were in your place," I suggested, "this is what I would do. I would use my selling ability to induce housewives to invite their neighbors in for a home-cooked dinner. I would cook that dinner with special aluminum cookware, and after the dinner was served, I would take orders for complete sets of the cookware used. If twenty guests were present, I feel sure I would sell half of them on purchasing my cookware."

"Very well," the soldier replied, "but where am I to sleep and what am I to eat while I am doing all this, not to mention where am I to get the money with which to purchase the cookware?"

Isn't it strange how the human mind often jumps to all the negatives, sums up all the obstacles which may be met with, when presented with an opportunity?

"Let me handle that," I replied. "Your job is to get yourself in a frame of mind in which you desire to become a multimillionaire by selling cookware. You do your job properly, and I will do mine. Did you hear of Henry Ford? Well, he founded and is operating the world's greatest industrial plant without money, without backers, without the sort of help I am offering you. And he had much less education than you had. And another thing I wish you to remember: Stop selling yourself short and begin believing you can do whatever you make up your mind to do!"

"While you are getting on your feet," I continued, "you will occupy the guest bedroom in my home. You may use my charge account at the Marshall Field's department store to outfit yourself with suitable clothing. And I will co-sign as security for the necessary stock of cookware you will begin with."

"Gee whiz!" he exclaimed. "You, a mere stranger, will do all this for me without knowing anything about me? Well, if you have that much faith in me, I sure believe I can do what you tell me to do."

"Now, that is the way I wish to hear you talk," I replied. "Let's be on our way home for dinner and more planning tonight."

"A swell break for a stranger to get!" do I hear you exclaim? No, a swell opportunity for me to share my blessings with others, thereby carrying myself one step nearer the peace of mind I was then seeking.

Near the end of this young man's first four years in selling aluminum cookware, he came back to see me and to pay up what he owed me. He handed me a blank check with his name signed to it and said, "Fill in whatever amount you desire, up to a million dollars."

He had taught others how to sell cookware by his methods, and through their services he had accumulated a little over $4,000,000, all of which he had in cash. I filled out the check for a modest $10,000, then handed it back to him to keep as a souvenir reminding him of the day he was introduced to himself—that self he had not seen before. And I was much nearer to the secret of peace of mind than I had ever been before.

This was the beginning of an extensive industry which now operates throughout the nation, selling aluminum and stainless-steel cookware by the method I taught this young soldier. One of my friends, Clarence Marsh, who manages the St. Louis branch of Century Metalcraft Corporation, selling cookware under this plan, has about 150 sales people working for him, not one of whom is earning less than $500 a month, and many are earning four times that amount, thanks to a plan I created for the purpose of helping a deserving young man to help himself.

So you see, when you break the ties that bind a human mind and introduce the owner of that mind to his real self, you not only come nearer to attaining peace of mind, but I fancy that the gates of hell shake with fear and the bells of heaven ring out with glory.

Yes, there is truly magic power in belief! That is why I admonish my friends to try it out and be convinced. Begin with belief in yourself. Follow through with belief in the greatest nation yet conceived by the mind of man, the good old USA. And lastly, remember that the freedom guaranteed to every citizen of this great nation is a necessary background for the attainment of peace of mind.

CHAPTER 3

CLOSE THE DOORS TO PAST UNPLEASANTNESS

The meaning of the word "transmute" is, in simple language,
"the changing or transferring of one element,
or form of energy, into another."
—NAPOLEON HILL

Nothing could be more dead than your past, so if you wish peace of mind, you must learn to close the doors to all past experiences which caused you grief. Digging up the sad experiences of one's past and dwelling upon them is worse than digging up dead cats.

Just remember that every unpleasant experience you ever had carried with it the seed of an equivalent pleasure or benefit. If you must think of these experiences, then learn to transmute them into something beneficial by searching for that seed of equivalent benefit. Perhaps the seed may consist in some useful lesson you could have learned only by sad experience.

What if the experience did leave ugly wounds in the heart? The seed of an equivalent benefit may consist in the fact that the heart has the power to heal all wounds, including still other wounds it may receive in the future.

Close the door on ugly experiences, disappointments, and frustrations. The Great Universal Healer, TIME, will not only heal the wounds, but it will also condition the mind to reveal the seed of an equivalent benefit available through these experiences.

When you close the door on any portion of your past which you do not wish to live over again, be sure to nail it down tight so you will not be tempted to peep through the crack to see what has happened to the experience you have discarded.

Remember, you are searching for the way to peace of mind! The path does not lead backwards through the graveyard of dead hopes and unpleasant experiences, a goodly number of which every human being experiences during a lifetime.

As the physical food you eat passes through your body, your system extracts from it those portions which are required for the health and maintenance of your body, discarding the remainder as waste, which must be eliminated before it becomes a deadly poison.

Your mind works in a similar manner in its reaction to the mental food you feed it through your daily experiences, some of which are good for your welfare and some of which must be eliminated before they, too, become deadly poisons.

When you have found peace of mind, your mind will automatically reject every thought and every mental reaction which is not beneficial for your welfare. Meanwhile, before you graduate into this desirable command of your mind, you will find it necessary to voluntarily throw off all negative mental influences which you do not want to become a part of your character.

The "throwing off" will consist in your forming the habit of transmuting all negative thoughts into positive reactions. "How is this done?" you ask. Simply by switching your thoughts away from the unpleasant experiences and directing them to pleasant circumstances. Let us demonstrate how this may be done by the following example:

You have suffered a bad disappointment through the failure of someone to reciprocate your love for that person. The wound is fresh and so deep you think it can never be healed. Perish that idea. "Never" is a long while. Start where you stand and redirect your love emotions to some other person. Then give TIME, the master healer, a chance to work for you. In a matter of days, or weeks at most, you will begin to wonder how you happened to be so fortunate as to have been forced to redirect your love emotions to a more welcoming, and perhaps more enchanting, person.

The alternate to this procedure—the one usually followed by those who never find peace of mind—is to hibernate in a period of brooding until you lose the better portion of your mind!

Close the door tightly on that old love, after you have taken inventory of it in retrospect and discovered that the seed of an equivalent benefit it yielded consists in the fact that it enriched your soul and forced you to seek and to find a greater love. No love experience ever is lost! For there is something in the mere expression of the emotion of love which forever enriches the soul of the lover, no matter whether or not the love is reciprocated.

Transmuted frustrations in love have been the great revealers of genius back through the ages of the past. And transmutations of other kinds of sad experiences likewise have brought to light geniuses who never would have been revealed without these experiences.

Thomas A. Edison's experience in having been expelled from school because his teacher believed he had an "addled" mind was the spark plug experience which touched off his hidden powers of genius and gave the world its greatest inventor.

O. Henry's one and only adventure in crime, which resulted in a prison sentence, was transmuted into the discovery of a talent as a writer which made him (Charles Porter) an immortal in the field of literature.

Jack London's frustrations during the early part of his life, including dead-end jobs, illness, and time in jail for vagrancy, were transmuted into novels which made him an international figure during his lifetime and for a long while thereafter.

Charles Dickens suffered a bad disappointment in connection with his first love affair. Instead of jumping off the highest building or taking an overdose of sleeping pills, he transmuted his unrequited love into his greatest literary work, *David Copperfield*, a masterpiece which opened to him a career which crowned him with both glory and riches fit for a king.

Abraham Lincoln, the Great Emancipator, was born in poverty and illiteracy and seemed destined, from the very beginning of his life, to suffer about every form of defeat known to man. He took up storekeeping but failed at this. He took up engineering, but the sheriff sold his surveying instruments for his debts. He took up law but won few cases. But the supreme tragedy of his life awaited him in the death of Ann Rutledge, the only woman he ever truly loved. That tragic experience reached deeply into the great soul of Lincoln and revealed to the world one of the great leaders of all times. He transmuted his greatest tragedy into his greatest success and became America's greatest president.

When you feel like "griping" because of some unpleasant experiences, change your mind and turn your attention to something over which you can express enthusiasm. This is transmutation which pays off handsomely.

CHAPTER 4

HOW TO TAKE POSSESSION OF YOUR MENTAL ATTITUDE

There is very little difference in people, but that little difference makes a big difference. The little difference is attitude. The big difference is whether it is positive or negative.

–NAPOLEON HILL

Your mental attitude, at any given time, is the focal point at which you may take full and complete control of your own mind and direct it to whatever ends you may desire, or, by neglecting to do so, permit it to lead you where you do not wish to go.

Your mental attitude is the floodgate, so to speak, through which you may control your mental reactions to all experiences, both the pleasant and the unpleasant. It is a safety valve provided by Nature as a means of control over one's entire mind power. It is the point at which one may pattern all plans for success, or, through neglect, permit failure to take over.

One's mental attitude may be controlled because of desire or motive. There are nine basic motives which are responsible for practically all of man's actions and deeds, by the use of which one's life is made to spell out S-U-C-C-E-S-S or F-A-I-L-U-R-E.

They are:

1. The emotion of LOVE

2. The emotion of SEX

3. The desire for MATERIAL GAIN (money)

4. The desire for SELF-PRESERVATION

5. The desire for SELF-EXPRESSION

6. The desire for FREEDOM OF BODY AND MIND

7. The desire for PERPETUTATION AFTER DEATH

And two negatives:

1. The emotion of ANGER AND REVENGE

2. The emotion of FEAR

Everything one does or refrains from doing voluntarily may be traced to one or more of these nine basic motives. Let us here emphasize the fact that peace of mind is attained only by the fullest exercise of the seven positive motives, never by the exercise of the two negative motives. Despite this truth, however, the vast majority of people are influenced throughout their lives by the two negative motives, thereby writing themselves a ticket for failure through the misguided application of their mind power, which would just as easily bring them success if their mental attitude were reversed from the negative to the positive.

If you would have peace of mind, suppress the two negative motives, or transmute your reaction to them into some form of positive endeavor, then make use of the seven positive motives as a means of keeping your mental attitude positive. You will not only find the true path to peace of mind, but you will achieve material success in whatever degree of abundance you demand.

You cannot have peace of mind while you fear anything or anyone. You cannot have peace of mind while you are motivated by the desire for revenge or the desire to injure another, no matter what the justification for that desire may be. "Whatsoever a man soweth that shall he also reap." All sowing takes place first in the mind of the individual through his mental attitude.

Great men have no time to waste on a desire to injure others. If they did have time to devote to this purpose, they would not be great men; they would be only the common, run-of-the-mill variety of which mankind in general consists in overwhelmingly large percentage, in comparison with those who attain greatness through self-discipline.

Your mental attitude is the thing which makes of your mind an attracting force which you experience throughout your lifetime. Because you can control your mental attitude, you can determine whether the things and circumstances you attract to yourself shall help or hinder you in finding peace of mind.

Your brain is constantly active, both while you sleep and while you are awake, broadcasting your own thought vibrations and picking up the vibrations being released by other brains! In picking up the thought vibrations being released by others, your brain selects those which harmonize with your own mental attitude. If your attitude is predominantly negative, it will attract kindred thoughts which you will mistake to be your own, and these negative thoughts will definitely give your mind a "no can do" mental attitude. If your mental attitude is dominated by some combination of the seven positive motives, it will attract to you kindred thought vibrations until your mental attitude becomes a "can do" power. Then you are "on the beam" and ready to carry out your plans with great success.

Also, you will have peace of mind.

Thoughts truly are things, and they come back to bless or to curse those who broadcast them, whether the release is voluntary or accidental. Henley had this truth in mind when he wrote:

I am the master of my fate:
I am the captain of my soul.

You may become the master of your fate, the captain of your soul, only by taking full possession of your own mind and focusing it on the positive motives which lead you directly to the things and circumstances of life you most desire, including peace of mind.

The privilege of such control is the only thing over which you have complete power. But it is sufficient for all your needs if you will make use of it.

You desire peace of mind, the greatest of all the riches available to man. Very well, start using the seven positive basic motives through which you may attract everything you need for peace of mind. And begin now, right where you stand.

> The surest way of finding peace of mind is that which helps the greatest number of people to find it.
>
> —NAPOLEON HILL

CHAPTER 5

BECOME ACQUAINTED WITH YOUR "INNER SELF"

The one and only person in all this world
through whose efforts you can be supremely
happy UNDER ALL CIRCUMSTANCES, and, through
whose labor you can accumulate all the material wealth
that you can use legitimately, is YOURSELF!
–NAPOLEON HILL

When you look into a mirror, you see only the house in which your real self lives. Sooner or later, the house will fall apart and go back to the dust from whence it came; the one who dwells there will go back to the eternal ocean of Infinite Intelligence from whence it came and become a part of that Intelligence, taking with it the benefits of a lifetime of human experience gained from the struggle of life.

Let us become better acquainted with that great, powerful entity that lives in the house you call your body, for it is the sole keeper of the secret of peace of mind. It is the maker of all your joys, all your sorrows; all your successes and all your failures; your sickness and your health; your miseries and your peace of mind.

This unseen entity which dwells within you carries out, to the finest detail, all instructions you give it, but it makes no attempt to determine for you the nature of those instructions. You are a free agent in the sight of this hidden entity, strictly on your own, with the power to shape and to direct your Inner Self to whatever ends you may desire. This profound prerogative is the only great asset you possess which you may control exclusively, and it is the one and only feature which distinguishes you from all other creatures on earth.

If your thinking is directed preponderantly to and about poverty, your Inner Self, or subconscious mind, will translate that thinking into terms of poverty. If thoughts of riches predominate your mind, the Inner Self will direct you unerringly to the ways and means of acquiring riches. These statements are no mere opinions of mine. They are well known to all scientific men and to many laymen as proven truths based upon inexorable laws of Nature.

Dr. Elmer R. Gates of Chevy Chase, Maryland, discovered this Inner Self and placed himself on such intimate terms with it that he could go into his "silence room" with any sort of mechanical or technical problem and come out with the solution a high percentage of times, often in a matter of minutes. In this manner, he perfected nearly three hundred patents, some of them basic.

The technique employed by Dr. Gates in directing his Inner Self is both interesting and informative. He built a special meditation room in his home and had it insulated with sawdust between two heavy walls so he could cut off most of the outside sounds. In this room, he placed a small wooden table and chair and on the table a pad of paper and some pencils.

When he had a problem he wished to submit to his Inner Self, he went into this soundproof room, shut off the electric lights, seated himself at the table with pencil and paper, focused his attention upon the problem at hand, shut off all other thoughts from his conscious mind, and waited for ideas to present themselves. Very often, the information he sought would present itself in a matter of minutes. Then he switched on the lights and wrote down whatever came into his mind.

In this manner, Dr. Gates had revealed to him, for example, the principle by which crewless boats could be guided from land by the means of light prisms. Undoubtedly, his discoveries in this field, which dated back to the late 1890s, were the forerunners of all the methods now used for robot guidance and radar.

Once when I was lecturing on the Science of Success at Harvard University, I described many of Dr. Gates's achievements in detail. At the end of the lecture, a student arose from his seat and asked, "Will you tell us why Dr. Gates died without having accumulated any money if he had the power of inner vision which you have described?"

Having been associated with Dr. Gates as his secretary for three and a half years, I had the answer to that question. "He not only died without having accumulated any money," I replied, "but you may be interested in knowing that while he lived, he seldom had enough money to take care of himself and his family. He did not accumulate money because he did not direct his mind toward the accumulation of money; he was not money conscious. Remember the Inner Self translates the dominating thoughts of an individual into their precise material equivalents. Dr. Gates could have accumulated millions of dollars had he desired to do so."

I was glad that question was asked as it provided me with an opportunity to emphasize the fact that not all success can be measured in terms of money. The training I received under Dr. Gates's guidance placed at my disposal the knowledge with which, many years later, I was able to influence Nature to restore 65 percent of the normal hearing capacity of my son Blair, who was born without ears or any part of the natural hearing equipment. I communicated with Blair's mind from the day he was born until nine years later, mainly through the medium of his subconscious mind, while he was asleep.

And I also gained, from my training under Dr. Gates, the knowledge which enabled me to write a lesson on Applied Faith, which has helped millions of people to discover and make use of their Inner Selves. Also, this training laid the foundation through which I finally found the true path to peace of mind which I am now revealing to you through these messages.

In relating my experience with Dr. Gates, I shall, in fairness to younger generations who may never have heard of him and his achievements, explain that he was one of the few great scientists produced by this country in the nineteenth century. He ranked high in the field of scientific research and had to his credit more inventions than those created by Thomas A. Edison.

And it was my training under Dr. Gates and Dr. Alexander Graham Bell which led me to the discovery of my famous self-guidance formula known as the Eight Princes, which I will describe in a later message in this series. Through the aid of these eight Princes my every need in life is automatically taken care of, while I am awake and while I sleep.

The names of these Princes are: FINANCIAL SERCURITY, SOUND PHYSICAL HEALTH, PEACE OF MIND, HOPE, FAITH, LOVE, ROMANCE, and OVERALL WISDOM. The names will suggest the nature of the service they render me. My sole compensation to these Princes, for their services, is unyielding gratitude.

CHAPTER 6

SO, YOU DESIRE A BETTER JOB

To be successful, you must find peace of mind, acquire the material needs of life, and above all, attain happiness. All of these evidences of success begin in the form of thought impulses.

—NAPOLEON HILL

You do not like your job because it pays too little and you have to work too hard for what you get. Is that something like your problem? Well, take heart and look to the future, for there is a way out for you, if you will follow instructions!

Let us begin where you now stand, assuming you are something like the two mice caught in a trap. They got into an argument as to which one would eat the cheese which enticed them into the trap. "You go ahead and eat the cheese," said the wise mouse. "All I want is a roadmap to lead me out of this trap."

Let us say that YOU are the wise mouse type. Let me tell you about another man who found himself right where you stand today, in a trap, in a job he did not like, looking for a way out. The roadmap he used to improve his position might serve you also. Here it is:

The story begins in the Foundry Department of the R. G. LeTourneau Company of Georgia, the most undesirable place to work in the entire plant because of the heat, smoke, and dirt. Twenty men worked in that department; one of them made up his mind to promote himself out.

Observing that nearly all the men working with him spent a large portion of each day "griping" about their unpleasant work, this man hit upon an idea which not only served to lift him out of his undesirable job, but it attracted to him bigger and better opportunities until finally one came which placed him in a successful business of his own which he now operates, with peace of mind thrown in for good measure.

One by one he sold his fellow workers in the Foundry Department the idea of looking for something about their jobs for which to be thankful and to express their gratitude in writing to management. The idea caught on like wildfire. Very soon there were no "gripes" coming out of the Foundry. Also, something strange happened in that department which lifted it out of the "red" in operating costs, where it had been for years, and made it one of the most profitable departments of the entire plant. Naturally, that led to increased pay for the workers.

The man who let loose this strange influence was promoted from one job to another until he reached the top with that company. Meanwhile, his reputation had spread throughout the community, and he began to get offers from the best-known concerns at wages such as he never had dreamed of receiving. One came from the telephone company. Another from the electric power company, and still another from a large furniture manufacturer.

A national magazine carried a story about this unusual man, who had made himself a reputation by the simple process of creating a positive atmosphere where he worked, and that story attracted to him a very wealthy man who put up the necessary working capital to start him in a manufacturing business of his own.

When I last talked with this man, I asked him if he could tell me, in one short sentence, what had brought about such a great change in his life. "Yes," he replied. "I think I can. I stopped looking at the hole in the doughnut and started looking at the doughnut instead." Very well stated. He changed his mental attitude, and everything affecting his entire life changed with it. This process is available to every man who is not satisfied with his lot in life and is willing to follow a sound philosophy in order to change his life.

Remember, the starting point is in one's own mind, where mental attitude can and must be controlled. Every job provides two benefits: one is the money that comes in the pay envelope; the other is the opportunity for a person to demonstrate his ability. The latter is the greatest asset of the two because it can be expanded into whatever one demands of life, while the former is limited by the competition of others engaged in the same sort of work.

Opportunity can be seized by anyone without the help or consent of others by the simple process of "Going the Extra Mile," as the Foundry worker did. That means rendering more service and better service than one is paid to render and doing it in an agreeable mental attitude. The man in a little job can, in this way, make himself so valuable that his employer cannot afford to keep him there. He is worth more in a bigger job, higher up the ladder.

Rarely do men make use of the principle of Going the Extra Mile as a blueprint into a bigger opportunity and greater compensation. The average man is something like the fellow whom Henry Ford once described to me. Mr. Ford interviewed a number of men for an important job he wished to fill. One of the applicants looked more promising than the others, so Ford asked how much salary he required, to which the man replied, "All I can get."

"Well," said Ford, "I do not know how much you are worth, and apparently you do not either, so suppose we arrange it this way: you go to work in the job and demonstrate your ability for a month, at the end of which we will put you on the payroll for all you are worth."

"Not on your life," the applicant exclaimed, "for I'm getting more than that where I now work."

Ford said that subsequent experience with this man proved that he had told the truth.

Peace of mind; a responsible, well-paying job or business; and success in the upper brackets are some of the rewards which come to the man who helps to enrich the lives and the minds of those around him by his own mental attitude. Andrew Carnegie once said that a man with a negative mental attitude would influence and discolor the minds of every man in the works, even though he never opened his mouth. On the other hand, he willingly paid Charles M. Schwab as much as $1,000,000 a year in extra compensation, over and above his regular salary, because of the fine quality of mental attitude which Mr. Schwab spread throughout the works with his personality.

Schwab's salary, at the peak of his association with Carnegie, was $75,000 a year. That was for the actual work he did. That he often received more than ten times this amount for the mental attitude he carried around with him was because his healthy state of mind benefited thousands of other workers in the Carnegie plants. And Schwab began as an ordinary laborer, at wages of fifty cents a day. He promoted himself into the biggest job in the works with the only thing he actually controlled—his own mind.

This concludes my series of messages on how to achieve peace of mind. Please put these lessons to use, and it will be within your reach.

PART
TWO

FORTUNE TO SHARE:
HOW TO ADAPT YOURSELF TO
THE LAW OF COMPENSATION

IF YOU ARE NOT A STUDENT OF EMERSON, now is the right time to become one. Start by reading his essay on Compensation, which is a "must" for the person who seeks peace of mind.

The first time you read this essay, you may not get much out of it, but wait until you have read it several times. Then you will begin to understand the futility of fretting over circumstances which you cannot control.

Also, you will learn that Nature's laws are fixed eternally. They cannot be circumvented or influenced in any manner by anyone, nor can they be suspended from operation by anyone for any purpose.

However, there is one benefit you may gain from Nature's immutable laws: you may adapt yourself to them and move in harmony with them and thus avoid the inevitable and unhappy consequences of ignoring those laws. You cannot push Nature's laws around, but you can get in front of them and let them push you around in the direction you wish to go if you are seeking peace of mind.

You would do well to recognize, here and now, that if you are to find peace of mind and retain it, you must become a philosopher. A philosopher is one who analyzes all things, including the circumstances which influence men's lives for weal or for woe, by causes and effects.

If the philosopher becomes physically ill, he seeks to know the cause of his ailment and the quickest way to remove it. If he seeks material riches, he searches for the causes which result in the accumulation of riches and makes use of those causes. If he meets with some form of disaster, he seeks the cause so as to avoid a repetition. If he desires peace of mind, he searches for all the factors which clear the way for peace of mind and adopts them as his own, which is what you presumably are doing by reading this essay.

The philosopher avoids most of the major causes of grief which overtake the majority of people because he constantly observes the mistakes of others and profits by them before they become his own experiences.

When the philosopher wishes to take a look into the future, he does not seek the aid of the stars, nor does he look into a crystal ball, but he takes inventory of the past, for he knows that history has a way of repeating itself.

And being a philosopher, he knows that every evil of whatever nature, and every circumstance which is not in harmony with Nature's overall plan for the operation of the universe, will be eliminated with TIME.

In his business dealings, the philosopher seeks no unfair advantage over others, not so much perhaps because of his inherent honesty as for his fear of the consequences. He knows that unfair bargains carry a penalty far out of proportion to any temporary benefits they may bring the man who indulges in them.

The philosopher knows that thoughts are things; that every thought he sends forth, whether it be good or bad, comes back in due time to curse or to bless him, according to its nature. Moreover, he knows that every thought sent forth comes back greatly multiplied and brings with it a large family of its relatives.

The philosopher knows that whatever he does to or for another he does to or for himself! Therefore, he clears the way for peace of mind by sharing his blessings with others. He knows full well that in every such circumstance he plants the seed of opportunity for self-benefit which will ripen into a rich harvest as surely as night follows day.

The true philosopher never slanders another person for any cause whatsoever. When he feels he must give expression to righteous indignation in connection with the faults of others, as all human beings do at times, he does not speak it; he writes it—writes it in the sand, near the water's edge. And he hopes that no man may pass that way until after the tide comes in.

The true philosopher never assumes the role of reformer, for he recognizes that genuine reformation must come from within the individual himself, inspired by his own desires, or forced by the penalties of his own errors. Moreover, he knows that some of the greater lessons of life, which everyone must learn for himself, come from the hurts of one's own mistakes and not through the counsel of others. Go back into your yesterdays and see if you do not find justification for this statement.

Every time I think of trying to reform someone, I dismiss the idea as quickly as possible and think of that experience during my youth when I paid a dollar for a bottle of beer on my first and last visit to a speakeasy. I thought the price would be a dime, the same as it was at the corner saloon. I know now that not all the sermons of the righteous against the evils of speakeasies could have served me as well as did that dollar investment, because a dollar was just a few dimes less than all the money I possessed.

Again, the philosopher knows that we "live and learn." If he is a truly deep philosopher, he perhaps believes that the major purpose of life is to give people an opportunity to learn from their own experiences as well as from their observations of the experiences of others. Stern lectures intended to reform rarely produce results.

When I think of the value of lessons learned from hard experiences, it reminds me of another experience I had when I was a very small boy. My grandfather took me with him on a trip down Powell's River, in Virginia, where he went with his horse-drawn wagon to bring back a load of hay. On our way back, a young smart aleck of the "city slicker" type jumped on the wagon and said, "Give us a ride, Hayseed." Grandfather made no reply. After we had reached Grandfather's place and began to turn into his barn, the young lad called, "Hey, how far is it to Big Stone Gap from here?" "Well," Grandfather replied, "if you start walking back the way we came, it is about 20 miles. If you keep on the way we were going, it is about 25,000 miles."

I shall never forget the expressions on that lad's face as he slid down from the pile of hay and started walking back the way he had come. I wondered then why he did not ask for information when he got on the wagon. I never learned why. But I learned not to repeat his mistake. All of which gives some idea of what a philosopher is and leads us up to some experiences of mine which aptly illustrate just how the Law of Compensation works out in the daily lives of people.

The arm of the Law of Compensation is very long. It takes no heed of impediments or of time. And it takes full account of every circumstance of an individual's life, of his every thought as well as all his deeds. Come; let us see how long was this arm in connection with one of my more recent personal experiences which involved the Law of Compensation.

Due to one of my adventures which brought me some valuable experience, but little else, I found it necessary to divest myself of all my material possessions and make a brand-new start, financially, mentally, and spiritually. Not an unusual experience, I will admit, as many another man has found himself in the same position, but that part of the experience which was unusual I will now relate in detail, as it involves the manner in which I adapted myself to the great universal Law of Compensation so that all of my losses were more than regained, with compound interest on compound interest, so to speak.

Let us take up the story at the beginning in the downtown business district of Atlanta, Georgia, where I was visiting my friend, Mark Wooding, a former business associate who had recently opened a large cafeteria in the very heart of the business section of the city.

Mark informed me that he was in serious difficulty with his business, due to his not having taken into account the fact that downtown Atlanta business houses close early each evening, after which the district in which he was located resembled a graveyard. His luncheon business was splendid, but business at his dinner hour, which should have been his most profitable, was negligible.

By the time he had finished his story, I had the answer to his problem. Wooding needed to provide the people with a motive for dining in the downtown business section, other than that of obtaining good food. They could get good food in many other parts of the city where business was still active during the evening or at home.

Like most people who are close to pressing problems, Mark's anxiety over his lack of business had prevented him from freeing his imagination long enough to enable it to find the answer to his problem.

I, too, had problems facing me—serious problems. But long before, I had learned that when one has a problem so great that he cannot find its solution, the best thing he can do is to look for someone with a greater problem and start helping him find its solution. That is precisely what I did after I heard Mark Wooding's story.

I looked around and noticed that he had a beautiful, large dining room in which he could seat several hundred people. His equipment was superb. It was a new place and was located on one of the best corners, near transportation and parking facilities. My imagination was not long in coming up with the answer to Mark's problem. I would simply put on a lecture course on my Philosophy of Individual Achievement and hold my classes nightly in Mark's dining room, the lectures to be given free to all who came for dinner and remained for the lectures. The dinner check was the admission ticket to the lectures.

Through the local newspaper we announced this plan. We also sent printed announcements to all of the business houses in the district. The first night, we turned away more than we could seat. And there was seldom a night thereafter that we did not turn away a large number. Mark's dinners became the major portion of his business in record time.

And the cost? Just the cost of the advertising. My services were donated without charge as my contribution to a friend who needed a helping hand, which I was prepared to lend him. Remember this point. It is an important part of this story.

Having helped my friend to solve his problem, I was well on the way toward the solution of my own, although I did not know it at the time, as no visible evidence of benefits to me had come to my attention. But let us observe how that long arm of the Law of Compensation works silently, often unnoticed. Let us remember, also, Emerson's profound admonition: "Do the thing and you shall have the power."

Well, I had "done the thing," and I had done it in a spirit of unselfishness, activated only by the desire to be helpful to my friend in a time of need. I never stopped to ask, "What will I get out of this?" It was compensation enough for me to have the privilege of rendering a real service to a deserving friend, with so little effort on my part. I was serving him because it gave me pleasure to serve. I was engaging in a labor of love, doing the thing I liked best to do.

If I could have read the crystal ball accurately at this point, I would have seen, in this service I had rendered my friend, the most important turning point of my entire life—a fact which very soon will be obvious to you. What was I to get out of my services? Only time will tell the complete story, for the payoff is still in progress.

Previous to that experience, for some time the hand of destiny had for me been stilled. Now it began to move again! And my star of Hope was once more in the ascendency. I had cured my own ills by helping a friend to cure his. If I can only get this point across to you who read this, you may well have cause to say that this essay has marked the most important turning point in your life. Remember:

I had cured my own ills by helping a friend to cure his! Repeat this line often, will you? And do something about it at your first opportunity. If no opportunity presents itself, make one! It will lead you a very long way in the direction of peace of mind, very close to the revelation of the supreme secret of peace of mind.

My lectures on the success philosophy at Wooding's restaurant attracted a wide variety of types of people, among them many top-ranking executives of downtown Atlanta businesses and industries. In the group was an executive of the Georgia Power Company who was so favorably impressed by the lectures that he extended me an invitation to be the guest speaker at a private meeting of the leading officials of several southern power companies.

At that meeting, the second of a series of dramatic episodes which would change my entire destiny revealed itself. After I had finished speaking to the power officials, Homer Pace, an executive of the South Carolina Power Company, introduced himself and informed me that he had been a student of my philosophy for many years.

"I have a friend," said he, "whom I wish you to meet. He is the president of a small college and owns a large printing establishment. He speaks your language so fully that I suspect he also is one of your students. I have a feeling that you two men should become associated in business. Write to him, won't you?"

I acted on his suggestion and sent the college president and publisher a brief note describing my conversation with the power company executive. He did not wait to answer my note in writing but went immediately to Atlanta to call on me. We talked for a couple of hours and then ended our visit with a verbal agreement by which I would move to his hometown and begin at once to rewrite my entire Philosophy of Success from the notes I had made during my personal conversations with my sponsor, Andrew Carnegie.

On the first of January, 1941, having moved to his hometown, I began work on seventeen volumes, under the title of *Mental Dynamite*, blissfully unaware that a silent, unseen figure stood at my back, looking over my shoulder as I worked and changing my destiny with every word I wrote.

For eleven continuous months I worked on those manuscripts as I had never worked at anything previously. I literally transmuted the shock of one of the worst experiences of my life, an unhappy divorce, into "Mental Dynamite," and little did I realize the far-reaching influence that this interpretation of my philosophy was destined to attain.

Unconsciously, I was experiencing the truth of a statement I had so often made during my lectures—that "Life never takes anything away from anyone without giving him something of equal or greater benefit in return."

I was still too close to the open wound of my hurt from my broken marriage to recognize its value in changing the course of my life. Having lost myself in the service of others, through the writing of the new manuscripts, I soon washed away my own disturbances of mind and cleared the way for peace of mind such as I had never known before.

Meanwhile, something of much greater benefit to me was edging its way into my life, without my recognizing it at the time. Before I describe this episode that was definitely to change the course of my life and which began with the complimentary service I had rendered my friend Wooding, please observe that my whole life had been thrown into my work. I was not seeking romance, and as far as the idea of marrying anyone again was concerned, that was something which couldn't happen, so I thought, which reminds me of that very aptly stated quotation: "Man proposes; God disposes."

I suspect that if the southern publisher could have foreseen the enfoldment of this episode before he brought me to this town as a business associate, he would never have made the deal with me. You will soon learn why.

Now comes the next payoff from the Law of Compensation, which was so adequately suited by its very nature to fill every vacuum in my life that had been left there by previous frustrations. When I moved to the little South Carolina town of Clinton to write these volumes, I had an apartment in the same house as did the publisher's private secretary. For the first several months after my arrival, I saw the secretary only at her office. In the office, I saw her many times daily, for I frequently had occasion to transact business through her.

She had been associated in the business with two generations of the publisher's family and had a very responsible position, in which she was quite happy. I am sure that marriage was the farthest thing from her mind in all her dealings with me. When she was quite young, her father passed away, leaving her as the "head of the family," and she assumed the responsibility of helping to educate her younger sisters. Between the family responsibilities and those of holding down an executive job, she had little time to think seriously about marrying anyone.

My relationship with the secretary began to take on a different trend after several months, for I occasionally invited her to drop her duties and accompany me to dinner and perhaps to a show in nearby towns. I discovered that the moment she shed her business dignity away from her office and got out from under the family responsibilities, she was quite a delightful personality.

In fact, I soon discovered that both in physical appearance and in personality, she was almost a perfect duplicate of the greatest woman who had ever entered my life—my stepmother. From that time on, the picture began to unfold rapidly. Motor trips on which she accompanied me became frequent occurrences. On Sunday mornings, we always attended the Mormon Tabernacle radio services when we were driving in the country.

Then came that historic day, December 7, 1941, when the Japanese forces struck Pearl Harbor. The impact of that shock on my publisher was so great that he brought our business arrangement to an abrupt end, and I left the South Carolina town to take over an important assignment with the R. G. LeTourneau Company in Georgia.

There I was destined to meet with the greatest opportunity of my life to demonstrate the soundness of my philosophy as a builder of harmonious relations between employers and their employees.

For almost two years, I had an unparalleled opportunity to share my blessings with the two thousand LeTourneau employees. I had carte blanche privileges in the LeTourneau plant, and I had to report to no one except myself.

With all due modesty, I can truthfully say that my influence in the LeTourneau plant changed for the better every person who worked there, including the top management. And in thus helping others, I laid the foundation for another move that was destined to pave the way for my philosophy to serve all industry as it had served the LeTourneau Company and its employees. That move called for a change of residence to Los Angeles, the capital city of talking picture productions.

The day before I left for the West Coast, I added the secretary in Clinton as a life member of my Master Mind group, in the capacity of my wife, my secretary, and my business associate. We are now entering the fourteenth year of this partnership, with an outlook of opportunity for service to mankind such as I never dreamed of experiencing.

I suspect that when I left South Carolina just after the Pearl Harbor attack, my publisher hardly thought I would return from Georgia and take away with me one of his greatest assets. And the irony of it all consists in the fact that he assisted in the marriage ceremony.

On a later visit to South Carolina, we saw the publisher for the last time. He was lying in a casket amid a great bank of flowers. As I stood there and looked at him in his last sleep, I could not help uttering a prayer of gratitude for his influence in changing the destiny of my life as well as that of my wife, for we have found peace of mind together sufficient to compensate for all of the hurts we have experienced in the past. Now we are engaged in a labor of love and are trying to help others to find the path to the Holy Grail of life.

Yes, the arm of the Law of Compensation is very long. Through four dramatic episodes, it reached all the way from Wooding's Cafeteria in Atlanta, Georgia, to Los Angeles. It is carrying me step by step onward to some as yet unknown destiny, where, I hope, I shall yet have greater opportunities to help men and women find peace of mind as well as material prosperity.

I have related this story in all of its essential details to show you how the Law of Compensation often works. It achieves objectives not by going directly from cause to effect but by the progressive method, as in my case—by taking one step at a time and changing course often.

Of all the places I know throughout the United States, that little town in South Carolina is the very last place I would have chosen voluntarily as a suitable place for recuperating from a mental setback. Yet, some invisible power silently guided me to that town and kept me there while I completed one of the most helpful of all my works on success philosophy, and that same power brought me one of my greatest blessings. Then, when the task was done, it just as silently picked me up and pushed me on to bigger and brighter opportunities.

This is but one of many similar experiences I have had which leads me to the conclusion that there are unseen, silent forces which influence all of us constantly. Some of these are positive; some are negative. Some are good for us; some are very harmful. The purpose of this essay is to undertake to show you how to choose the friendly forces from among the unfriendly and how to make the favorable forces your allies.

Of course I am fully aware that there are some who may criticize me for the very personal references described in this essay, but this does not disturb me in any way—no more, in fact, than if I had resorted to the technique so often used by my friend, the late Edward Bok, editor of *Ladies' Home Journal*, who got across his ideas by writing letters to himself on controversial subjects using pseudonyms and then answering them in the columns of his magazine.

Just after the close of World War II, I saw a book entitled, *I Write As I Please*. I liked the title very much, provided it stated the truth, for any man who dares to write as he pleases has already gone a great distance toward attaining peace of mind, based upon the sort of personal freedom which all men covet. I suspect that much of what is written for publication on most subjects is written to please the reader, by pandering to his established prejudices and beliefs, more than to express the truth as the writer may see it.

There was a time when an impressive corps of critics went over every line I wrote before my writings got into print. That time has passed. I now write "as I please" and let the chips fall where they may.

Now let us have a brief visit with Ralph Waldo Emerson, through his essay on Compensation. Such a visit reveals to us important truths leading in the direction of peace of mind through a better understanding of Nature's laws.

Every act rewards itself, or, in other words, integrates itself in a twofold manner; first, in the thing, or, in real nature; and secondly, in the circumstance, or in apparent nature. Men call the circumstance the retribution. The causal retribution is in the thing, and is seen by the soul. The retribution in the circumstance is seen by the understanding; it is inseparable from the thing, but is often spread over a long time, and so does not become distinct until after many years. The specific stripes may follow late after the offense, but they follow because they accompany it. Crime and punishment grow out of one stem. Punishment is a fruit that unsuspected ripens within the flower of the pleasure which concealed it. Cause and effect, means and ends, seed and fruit, cannot be severed; for the effect already blooms in the cause, the end preexists in the means, the fruit in the seed.[1]

If you reduce the preceding paragraph from the abstract language in which it is expressed and restate it in concrete terms, you will have a perfect analysis of the four episodes in my life which began at Wooding's in Atlanta. The cause behind these episodes consisted in a simple act of service rendered to a friend who was in need. The effect, four times removed from the cause, gave me a firm footing on the very foundation of everything that leads to peace of mind.

In the following paragraph Emerson expresses his understanding of that silent unseen power to which I have previously referred:

Men suffer all their life long, under the foolish superstition that they can be cheated. But it is as impossible for a man to be cheated by any one but himself, as for a thing to be, and not to be, at the same time. There is a third silent party to all our bargains. The nature and soul of things takes on itself the guaranty of the fulfillment of every contract, so that honest service cannot come to loss. If you serve an ungrateful master, serve him the more. Put God in your debt. Every stroke shall be repaid. The longer the payment is withholden, the better for you; for compound interest on compound interest is the rate and usage of this exchequer.[2]

And again, in the following paragraphs Emerson offers encouragement to the person who has not yet learned that every adversity carries with it the seed of an equivalent benefit:

The changes which break up at short intervals the prosperity of men are advertisements of a nature whose law is growth. Every soul is by this intrinsic necessity quitting its whole system of things, its friends, and home, and laws, and faith, as the shell-fish crawls out of its beautiful but stony case, because it no longer admits on its growth, and slowly forms a new house....

And yet the compensations of calamity are made apparent to the understanding also, after long intervals of time. A fever, a mutilation, a cruel disappointment, a loss of wealth, a loss of friends seems at the moment unpaid loss, and unpayable. But the sure years reveal the deep remedial force that underlies all facts. The death of a dear friend, wife, brother, lover, which seemed nothing but privation, somewhat later assumes the aspect of a guide or genius; for it commonly operates revolutions in our way of life, terminates an epoch of infancy or of youth which was waiting to be closed, breaks up a wonted occupation, or a household, or style of living, and allows the formation of new ones more friendly to the growth of character. It permits or constrains the formation of new acquaintances, and the reception of new influences that prove of the first importance to the next years; and the man or woman who would have remained a sunny garden flower, with no room for its roots and too much sunshine for its head, by the falling off the walls and the neglect of the gardener, is made the banyan of the forest, yielding shade and fruit to wide neighborhoods of men.[3]

If Emerson had not written the preceding lines long before I was born, I might well believe he was writing directly to me, for the philosophy he has expressed fits my experiences perfectly. And my experiences have proven the soundness of Emerson's philosophy.

Emerson's views on the subject of fear, as expressed in the following paragraph, were responsible for a self-imposed house cleaning that I engaged in many years ago, by which I removed from my mind all breeding places for fear in all of its forms:

Fear is an instructer of great sagacity, and the herald of all revolutions. One thing he always teaches is that there is rottenness where he appears. He is a carrion crow, and though you see not well what he hovers for, there is death somewhere. Our property is timid, our laws are timid, our cultivated classes are timid. Fear for ages has boded and mowed and gibbered our government and property. That obscene bird is not there for nothing. He indicates great wrongs which must be revised.[4]

And whatever tendency I may have had toward envy of seemingly more fortunate persons, that tendency was eliminated through the influence of the following paragraph from Emerson's essay on Compensation:

Every excess causes a defect; every defect an excess. Every sweet hath its sour; every evil its good. Every faculty which is a receiver of pleasure has an equal penalty put on its abuse. It is to answer for its moderation with its life. For every grain of wit there is a grain of folly. For everything you have missed, you have gained something else; and for everything you gain, you lose something. If riches increase, they are increased that use them. If the gatherer gathers too much, nature takes out of the man what she puts into his chest; swells the estate, but kills the owner. Nature hates monopolies and exceptions. The waves of the sea do not more speedily seek a level from their loftiest tossing than the varieties of condition tend to equalize themselves. There is always some leveling circumstance that puts down the overbearing, the strong, the right, the fortunate, substantially on the same ground with all others.[5]

It was the preceding paragraph from Emerson's works which turned me back from the false notion of seeking success through the accumulation of "things" and started me on the higher road to success by rendering useful service and thereby placing people in my debt without demanding or expecting payment except by the voluntary will of the debtor. This put me on the path to peace of mind.

Although I have tested Emerson's views on the Law of Compensation by my own experiences and found them based upon eternal truth, I suspect that you will not get the full benefit of his philosophy except by measuring your own experiences with it. And unless you are much keener of mind than I was during my first reading of Emerson's works, I imagine you will look upon them as a sort of abstract preachment on the moral laws of life.

When you study Emerson's essays, you will begin to think along a new path. You will be forced to do so if you are to understand his writings. Before you may enjoy peace of mind to the fullest, you must learn to think for yourself. Secondhand clothes can be worn; secondhand automobiles can be driven, but secondhand thoughts are either worthless or dangerous.

"Beware," said Emerson, "when the great God lets loose a thinker on this planet. Then all things are at risk. It is as when a conflagration has broken out in a great city, and no man knows what is safe, or where it will end. There is not a piece of science, but its flank may be turned tomorrow; there is not any literary reputation, not the so-called eternal names of fame, that may not be reviled and condemned. The very hopes of man, the thoughts of his heart, the religion of nations, the manners and morals of mankind, are all at the mercy of a new generalization."[6]

Yes, men who think for themselves determine the trend of our civilization. This has always been true; it will always be true. The only free men are those who have learned how to think for themselves.

After I had milked the works of Emerson dry, I was still thirsty for more of the truth he so definitely expressed. My thirst led me, eventually, to the revelation of Nature's greatest law, the law which serves as a comptroller of all natural laws. I have named it the Law of Cosmic Habitforce. It takes in all that Emerson has described in his essay on Compensation and much more which he had not uncovered. But it was Emerson's essay on Compensation which sent me on the prowl, in search of something which I recognized he had not discovered, and I found it.

NOTES

1. Ralph Waldo Emerson, "Compensation," *Essays* (Boston: James Munroe and Co., 1841), 85.

2. Ibid., 98.

3. Ibid., 102–04.

4. Ibid., 92.

5. Ibid., 81–82.

6. Ralph Waldo Emerson, "When God Lets Loose a Thinker," *Busy Man's Magazine*, November 1, 1908, https://archive.macleans.ca/article/1908/11/1/when-god-lets-loose-a-thinker.

THREE

HILL'S GOLDEN RULE MAGAZINE

THE SCANDALMONGERS

JANUARY 1919

If you must slander someone, don't speak it,
but write it in the sand, near the water's edge.

The most dangerous reptile that crawls around over this old earth is not the thick, flat-headed, venomous snake, but the stealthy, cunning human reptile whose tongue wags, without restraint, at both ends!

Sometime ago my secretary called a man on the telephone and intended to make an appointment for him to see me. I had in mind employing this man, and the position would have paid $3,000 a year, or more!

Before the appointment was negotiated, however, the name of a man whom this applicant knew was mentioned, and immediately he began to vilify and denounce him. He was "a rogue, a thief and a liar!" Nothing was too mean to be said about him. When my secretary reported to me what had happened, I cancelled the engagement with this man, because it so happened that the man he so vehemently denounced was my close personal friend, and I knew there was not a word of truth to what this other man had said about him.

Just to satisfy my curiosity I called this friend of mine on the telephone and asked him what he knew about the party who had so stoutly denounced him. This is what I learned (without telling my friend what the other man said about him)—that he had never met this man in his life—that one of his acquaintances, with whom he had had a misunderstanding in business and whom he had been compelled to sue for damages, was a brother-in-law of the man.

I then called this man on the telephone and asked him where he got his information about my friend, and, when I forced him into the corner, he admitted that all he knew was hearsay!

The power of suggestion is a wonderful power. It requires a strong will power to resist and refuse to accept even the slightest suggestion derogatory to another's character. Many an innocent woman's reputation has been smirched just by the nod of the head or a wink by a vulgar youth standing on the street corner.

I know from actual experience how hard it is to refrain from saying things about people that had best be left unsaid. Not until the past five or six years have I learned to curb my own tongue and to hear the names of those whose skeletons I might drag out mentioned without turning my tongue loose on them.

You know John Brown. You know something about his domestic or private affairs which might embarrass him in the eyes of his acquaintances if you were to speak. It is hard to refrain from speaking. I know just how hard it is, but bear in mind that maybe John Brown knows something concerning your record that you would not exactly enjoy having spread before your friends and acquaintances, as a morbid scandal feast! When you feel inclined to speak or even suggest anything that might hurt another's pride or character, just place yourself in his position, and imagine that the fellow whom you are about to assail is YOU!

Then you'll see how different it is!

Few people there are who haven't some little incident in their lives that they do not wish to have spread before the public. No man has the right to drag out the family skeleton of an acquaintance and exhibit it to the public.

It isn't good salesmanship, anyway!

The world hates a gossip. The fellow who will listen to your tale of scandal will think less of you thereafter! And, if he is the right sort of a person, he will avoid you, because he will know that "a dog that will bring a bone will take one away."

It cannot profit you to say an unkind word against any person, even though you may be warranted in doing so! The reason is that you not only lower yourself in the estimation of the person to whom you speak, but you demoralize YOURSELF in your own estimation, whether you realize it or not.

Every time you give away to that inherent disposition of human nature to speak in cynical, vulgar terms of your fellowmen, you add another brick to the building of your negative qualities. You remove yourself just that much farther away from that state of sereneness— that disposition of sweetness toward humanity that you hope sometime to attain!

Also bear in mind that a man never sinks so low but that there is much good in him, if it is developed and brought out. The best way in this world to bring out the good there is in a man is to let him know that you believe in him—give him a good reputation and he will do his best to live up to it. On the other hand, take a man whose purpose in life is lofty and ideal and constantly hound him and denounce him, and the chances are that, unless he has a remarkably strong will power, he will eventually accept the suggestion which you place in his mind and ACT THE PART which you have allotted to him.

Who are you, anyway, that you should set yourself up as a censor of human character? That's a question we should all ask ourselves! If you wish to vilify, defame and criticize any man, first turn the limelight on yourself and see what you can find there which those whom you are criticizing might find fault with if they were not more charitable than you are.

Furthermore, the loose tongue habit is a dangerous one for reasons other than those mentioned. A few months ago a man sat at a table in one of Chicago's restaurants. Two young men came in and sat down at the same table. Presently, one of them saw a young lady come in, and before they had time to see where she was going to sit down, one of them made an ugly remark about her. The man who sat at the table with them got up, picked up his chair and knocked the young man, who made the remark, senseless, and probably would have choked him to death had others not interfered and prevented it. The young lady who came in was this man's daughter. Investigation proved that the young man who made the remark did not personally know the young lady.

There's always a chance that you'll get your neck broken for making remarks about other people, even though they may be truthful remarks.

If you are a man of wealth, there is a chance also that you may have to pay a heavy indemnity in the nature of a judgment for slander, if you make remarks about other people.

But these are not the chief reasons why you ought to curb your tongue. The main reason why you should do so is that every time you let it run wild you make it that much harder to become a worthwhile, clean, high-minded person! You are building up that side of yourself which you ought to be restraining and holding in check.

All that any person has is his or her reputation. If you are the means, directly or indirectly, of despoiling that reputation, you are a THIEF of the worst sort. No porch climber can be compared to the person who would deliberately, with malice aforethought, destroy another's reputation.

It takes a lifetime to build a solid reputation, and when you steal that which another has worked a lifetime to build up, you are the worst serpent that crawls on the earth!

(Of course, I do not use the word YOU in a personal sense.)

A person may steal my fortune, but I'll soon have another, if he lets my reputation alone! Fortunes are built out of good reputations. Paupers are made out of bad reputations.

The next time you find yourself about to give way to the temptation to say something derogatory concerning someone that you know, bite the end of your tongue off rather than say it!

Do this and you'll feel the warm glow of satisfaction spread over your whole body the minute you do it! I know, for I have tried this myself. The satisfaction that comes to the person who might have defamed an acquaintance but didn't is one that will bring happiness and self-respect!

Learn the art of forgiving and forgetting!

If someone does you an injustice, by act or words, forgive and forget! Harboring a grudge against someone only poisons your own mind and discolors your own disposition so that it is unattractive.

When you learn to forgive, when you learn to abolish hatred, when you learn to throttle your tongue, when you feel inclined not to make uncomplimentary remarks concerning others, you will have learned how to be happy and how to be loved by all with whom you come in contact.

How much better, when talking to another person, to speak of the good qualities in those absent ones whose names you discuss, rather than the bad qualities, or what you believe to be their bad qualities. When another starts to vilify the name of an acquaintance, in talking to you, shift the conversation as soon as you can. Turn it toward more savory subjects!

You cannot make another person think well of you merely because you speak ill words of someone you know. You may poison another's mind against someone, but the chances are that his mind will also be poisoned against you at the same time.

You reap that which you sow! Then sow words of kindness, good cheer—words that make people happy! Acquire the habit of doing this and you will have gone a long way toward pulling the wild oats out of your own field of life.

No one ever spoke of another in vulgar terms but that a feeling of remorse and regret crept over him as soon as he did it. The scandalmonger knows he is doing wrong. His conscience tells him that! Listen to the small, still voice and let it guide you in your remarks concerning others.

This habit, if practiced, will bring to you life's richest blessings—it will help you to be happier because it will give you greater self-respect.

If I were to be asked to take some minister's pulpit for a day, and I knew that it would be my last chance to preach a sermon, I would take as my text the subject that I have written about in this "visit."

The man who would manage others must first learn to manage himself—particularly his own tongue!

A positive mental attitude can clear away all obstacles which stand between you and your major purpose in life.

THE BROAD-MINDED MAN

APRIL 1919

One of the best compliments that can be paid to a man is to say he is broad-minded. One of the most serious criticisms of a man is to say he is narrow-minded. This would not be so if these were fixed mental states which a man cannot change, like a bent for music, literature, mechanics, salesmanship, executive work or generalship. Compliment and criticism are the universal testimony that breadth of mind is a matter of the will and that a man can be broad-minded if he wills to do so. The true meaning of the term—being "broad-minded"—is this: holding the mind open for all the conclusions on slight evidence; not being influenced by prejudices, but giving every man the benefit of the doubt; being disposed to see the good in a man or a thing; making adequate allowances for conditions. Narrow-mindedness means just the opposite of this—letting prejudice dictate one's decisions and attitudes; looking for the evil in men and things and overlooking the good; never willing to let the germ of possibility develop into maturity; measuring all new things by old standards; having a ready classification for every new thing; being impatient to even hear of that which differs from one's fixed opinion.

Any person can choose which of these attitudes will dominate his life as surely as he can choose which book he will read, which key he will touch on the piano, or which kind of food he will order for his dinner.

"With all thy faults I love thee still." Thus sings the poet, and we call him sentimental; that is, at first thought we do. But upon second thought we change our minds. We then find that faults and defects are always in the minority and that the larger part of human nature is so wonderful and so beautiful that it must inspire admiration and love in everybody. With all their defects there is nothing more interesting than human beings; and the reason is that for every shortcoming in man there are a thousand admirable qualities. The poet, being inspired by the sublime vision of truth, can see this; therefore, what can he do but love? Whenever his eyes are lifted and whenever his thoughts take wings, his soul declares with greater eloquence than ever before, "What a piece of work is man!" Thus every moment renews his admiration, and every thought kindles the fire of his love.

When the ancient Latins wanted to say "bad, worse, worst," they put it "malus, pejor, pessimus." The superlative degree in three syllables sounds so good to express the most deplorable that we have tacked it onto the fellow who is the "limit" in always looking on the dark side of things.

The pessimist of modern days, chronically afflicted with gloomy forebodings, goes slouching up the boulevards and down the back alleys as he did along the highways and byways of Rome, and bears the same label. The corners of his mouth are on the nether slant. He carries an umbrella of long-faced melancholy to keep off the sunshine. He hates the bright side of the street and throws wet blankets upon enthusiasm. Everything that's handed him he thinks a lemon and drinks no sugar in his 'ade.

Would you marry one? Would you have one as a business partner? Would you eat with one and expect to entertain health at the same table? He is the human fly in the ointment of cheerful living.

SELF-CONTROL

AUGUST 1919

Before you can control conditions,
you must first control yourself. Self-mastery is
the hardest job you will ever tackle.

A few days ago, a wealthy man telephoned the electric light company to send down an electrician to turn on the lights in a new house which he had just rented to a new tenant. It was after hours and the workmen did not want to go out, but finally one man was persuaded to go, after he was told that the people who had just moved in were without light.

By the time the electrician got to the house, the wealthy man who owned it had managed, with his new tenant, to find the gas jets and light them. When the electrician saw that the house was lighted, he did not stop to ask any questions but started in to curse the wealthy man for bringing him away from his family under misrepresentations. He completely lost his equilibrium and called the wealthy man about everything he could think of. The wealthy man merely smiled and said to the irate workman: "You didn't give me time to explain that we found the gas and turned it on just before you got here." He then called his chauffeur, took the angry workman by the arm, and said, "Drive the gentleman home."

We of course have no way of reading a man's mind, at least not minutely; but we'll wager a few cigars that the workman felt mighty small as he climbed into the automobile of the man whom he had given every reason to feel insulted at his outburst of anger and lack of self-control.

As the wealthy man walked back to the house and joined his wife and the new tenant, whom he was helping to get settled in his new quarters, he merely said: "I had a regular spitfire to deal with, didn't I?" He showed no signs of anger. If he felt any, he carefully concealed his feelings. His name is well known from coast to coast. Self-control is one of the virtues which most people do not know that this man possessed. We have a strong leaning toward the belief that this self-control is largely, if not entirely, responsible for his immense fortune and his success in other directions.

If you wish to exercise any degree of control over others, you must first learn to exercise control over yourself. A man who "loses his temper" never can become a big leader. He never can have a large following of friends. The man who permits another to draw him into a controversy which causes him to lose his self-control is allowing that person to dominate him. When a person speaks to you with a snarl in his voice and frown on his face, reply in a soft, rich tone, with a smile on your face, and you take the wind out of his sails. You will be fencing with him with a weapon with which he is not familiar; consequently, you are sure to best him in the finale.

It is a hard matter to act so mean that no one else can go you one better. It is a hard matter to say ugly words which cannot be duplicated or excelled by another. But, when you exercise complete self-control and deal with an angry person with kindness and politeness, you are making use of a force and of a weapon with which most people are not as familiar as they should be; consequently, you win with hands down.

This writer once lost his temper over the poor service which a janitor was giving and went down into the basement into that gentleman's abode to unload onto him some good advice. After we had relieved our system of the load which we carried down for the janitor, he straightened himself up from the furnace which he was feeding, wiped the sweat from his coal-bespattered brow, and with a smile on his face, said: "You all are somewhat excited today, aren't you?" We all were! We were ashamed that we were, but so we were! We knew that the janitor, for the time being at least, was the more self-controlled man of the two, and it made us feel ashamed to have to admit it to ourselves, much less apologize to the janitor, which we finally summoned up the courage to do after we had gone back upstairs, thought the matter over and went down to the basement again.

There is nothing which that janitor would not do for us today, because, as he himself stated it, "we were big enough to apologize, even to a poor janitor, when we knew we were in the wrong."

We are glad of that difficulty with the janitor. It taught us one more lesson on the value of self-control.

It hurt our pride to go back down into that basement and apologize, but the feeling of satisfaction which came over us, as we saw from the expression on his face that we had regained his respect, was worth all the humiliation it cost us. Have you ever apologized to someone for some wrong you have done him in the past? There is a great feeling of satisfaction, accomplishment and peace of mind from having apologized when you knew you were in the wrong.

FREE THOUGHT AND THE HUMAN MIND

AUGUST 1919

Any influence which restrains a human being from making his own deductions, based upon the sense impressions which he received through his five senses of seeing, hearing, smelling, tasting and feeling, is a bad influence and works in opposition to progress of the human race.

The human race is rapidly cutting the fetters of dogmas and creeds which deny people the right to do their own independent thinking. If you doubt this, take an inventory in your own neighborhood of the people who once attended church but who have given up the habit. Interview a few of them and find out why they do not attend church anymore. Many will not admit it, but those who have the courage to do so will tell you frankly that they do not wish to act as hypocrites, and not being able to accept the whole of the creed imposed upon them by the church, they simply dropped out.

The mind of the human race demands room for development, exercise and growth. Deny it this right and you are working against the laws of Nature; consequently, you are bound to fail.

We claim no special insight into God's secrets, if in fact He has such a thing as a real secret, but we have a strong notion that He did not create men with the object of subjugating one to another, or with the intention of having one throw fear into the hearts of others with the threat of hell-fire! If your God burns up human beings, condemning them to everlasting torture for their ignorance and their lack of strength with which He built them, then your God is not the one we worship.

Our God loves the human race, all! The only punishment he permits to be inflicted upon any of the human family is that which we inflict upon ourselves, by our own acts, either willful or ignorant. Our God does not throw fear into His children's hearts, and He does not authorize anyone else to do so. Our God placed us on this earth, not to punish, defraud, defame, blackguard or annoy our brothers, but to extend the hand of brotherly love and to help make the journey through life as pleasant as possible.

We hope that you love Our God because we cannot love yours unless He is as kind as ours. We cannot love a cruel God or one which teaches us not to read His handwriting, which we may see in every blade of grass, every stone, every flowing brook, every tree, every flower, every bird, and every human being. If your God teaches you to deprive your fellowmen of their right to think for themselves, we cannot accept Him.

We hope that Your God is the same as ours. We do not know what the human mind is, but we do know that it is the cause of every bodily movement of the human being. We do know that it is a marvelous force which does not exist in any other form.

We also know that the human mind creates pretty much any condition in life which it can imagine, from which we feel justified in presuming that it savors somewhat of the Divine spark which touches the ether, the world and all that is in it, at every point and in every nook and corner.

Paint in your mind a picture of that which you want and Nature can and will help you get it if you keep that picture alive and do all that you know to do to transform the picture into concrete form. There is no mistake about this, but the person who has been taught not to think for himself is not likely either to believe this or to try to make use of the principle.

Prison walls are not the only places within which human beings are imprisoned. Indeed, there are worse forms of imprisonment outside of prison walls than there are inside of them. The person who is shut off, by superstition, false teaching, creeds and dogmas, from independent thinking is in a far more deplorable prison than the man inside of prison walls who still exercises his God-given right to think thoughts which are based upon what he can see, taste, smell, touch and hear.

We do not know what will happen after we leave this planet; neither does anyone else know, but we have a right to guess that if God really does punish people for their wrongdoings, He will not overlook the chap who throws fear into another's heart or restrains him from thinking independently.

If you want to fill your churches—to fill them with the very salt of the earth, the very pick of humanity—drop your clap-trap about God condemning poor, weak, human beings to everlasting flames and begin to teach Applied Psychology instead. Teach your followers that God gave them the most precious gift within His power—the gift of the human mind, with which they can create on this earth any sort of an environment they wish. Teach them that any concept, combination of concepts, thoughts or ideas which are placed in the human mind and held there will eventually begin to take on concrete form and shape. Teach them that God gave them that wonderful workshop which reposes within their hearts and brains—that wonderful architect which creates everything that man builds—with the intention of having them use and develop it to a higher and higher state until the human race completely breaks the chain which binds it to the animal stage of evolution.

We will lay you a bet at any odds that the first minister who does this will have to build new pews to accommodate people in his community who never were inside of his church before, and another bet that a minister who preaches the Golden Rule as it applies to business and to the relationship among men and women here on earth will find a ready and willing audience which will fill his Church to the overflowing and keep it filled.

Quit preaching fear! We do not like it. We are beginning to think for ourselves and your fear doctrine does not square up with that which we reason out for ourselves when we begin to think.

There may have been a time in the process of evolution of the human race when the doctrine of fear was essential to hold the animal-like tendencies of human beings in check. If so, it no doubt was during that period when men and women were unable to think intelligently and reason from cause to effect. It was during that period when the removal of the civilized human being from the Stone Age was but a short distance. It may be that fear was then needed as a help to evolution. But, if that need ever existed at all, it surely does not exist now. Time has softened the human heart and rendered it less violent. We restrain ourselves now because we are beginning to learn, through thought, that self-restraint gives us greater power and more happiness.

And, if a humble newspaper man may presume to suggest to you gentlemen of the ministry, do you not believe it would be a pretty good plan to commence showing men and women how to be happy here on this earth, right now, instead of devoting all of your energies to showing them how to save their souls in the world to come?

Think it over, gentlemen! Think it over! You cannot possibly damage your followers by inducing them to make use of the Golden Rule philosophy in their dealings with one another, here on this earth, and may it not be possible that you might do them a great deal of good?

DESIRE

SEPTEMBER 1919

Every adversity, every failure, every heartbreak,
carries with it the seed of an equal or greater benefit.

In every normal mind a sleeping genius lies, waiting for the gentle touch of strong desire to arouse it and put it into action!

Listen, you sorrow-laden brothers who are groping for the pathway which leads out of the darkness of failure into the light of achievement—there is hope for you.

It makes no difference how many are the failures you have undergone or how low you may have fallen; you can get on your feet again! The person who said that opportunity never knocks but once was woefully mistaken. Opportunity stands at your door day and night. True, she does not hammer at your door or try to break in the panels, but she is nonetheless there.

What if you have undergone failure after failure? Every failure is but a blessing in disguise—a blessing that has tempered your metal and prepared you for the next test! If you have never undergone failure, you are to be pitied, for you have missed one of Nature's great processes of true education.

What if you have erred in the past? Who of us has not done the same? Find the person who has never erred and you will find also a person who has never done anything worth mentioning.

The distance from where you now are to the place where you wish to be is but a hop, skip and jump! Possibly you have become a victim of habit and like many another, you have become enmeshed in a mediocre life-work. Take courage—there is a way out! Perhaps fortune has passed you by and poverty has you within its grip. Take courage—there is a pathway to happiness and peace of mind you can use intelligently and for your own good, and the chart of that pathway is so simple that we seriously doubt that you will make use of it. If you do, however, you are sure to be rewarded.

The forerunner to all human accomplishment is desire! So powerful is the human mind that it can produce the wealth you desire, the position you covet, the friendship you need, the qualities which are necessary for achievement in any worthwhile undertaking.

There is a difference between "wish" and "desire," in the sense that we are here referring to it. A wish is merely the seed or germ of the thing wished for, while strong "desire" is the germ of the thing desired, plus the necessary fertile soil, the sunshine and the rain needed for its development and growth.

Strong desire is the mysterious force which arouses that sleeping genius reposing in the human brain and puts it to work in earnest. Desire is the spark which bursts forth into a flame in the boiler of human effort and generates the steam with which to produce action!

Many and varied are the influences which arouse desire and put it to work. Sometimes the death of a friend or relative will do it, while at other times financial reverses will have the right effect. Disappointment, sorrow and adversities of every nature serve to arouse the human mind and cause it to function through new channels. When you come to understand that failure is only a temporary condition which arouses you to greater action, you will see, as plainly as you can see the sky on a clear day, that failure is a blessing in disguise. And, when you come to look upon adversity and failure in this light, you will begin to come into the greatest power on the face of this earth. You will then actually begin to make capital out of failure instead of allowing it to drag you down.

There is a happy day coming in your life! It is going to arrive when you discover that whatever you aspire to accomplish depends, not upon others, but upon you! The arrival of this new day will be preceded by your discovery of the strength of desire! And this new day will be filled with whatever you desire most, be it money, love, the satisfaction of serving others, or perhaps the supreme goal, peace of mind.

Start in right now, today, to create a strong and irrepressible desire for the station in life which you wish to attain. Make that desire so full and complete that it will absorb most of your thought. Dwell upon it by day and dream about it by night. Keep your mind focused on it during every spare moment. Write it out on paper and place it where you can see it at all times. Concentrate your every effort toward its realization, and lo!, as if in response to the touch of a magic wand, it will materialize itself for you.

The starting point of all achievement is desire.
Keep this constantly in mind. Weak desires bring about
weak results, just as a small fire makes a small amount of heat.

LEARN HOW TO USE THAT WONDERFUL MIND OF YOURS

OCTOBER 1919

The human mind is a composite of many qualities and tendencies. It consists of likes and dislikes, optimism and pessimism, hatred and love, constructiveness and destructiveness, kindness and cruelty. The mind is made up of all these qualities and more. It is a blending of them all, some minds showing one of these qualities dominating and other minds showing others dominating.

The dominating qualities are largely determined by one's environment, training, associates and particularly by one's own thoughts! Any thought held constantly in the mind, or any thought dwelt upon through concentration and brought into the conscious mind, often attracts to it those qualities of the human mind which it most resembles.

A thought is like a seed planted in the ground in that it brings back a crop after its kind, multiplies and grows. Therefore, it is dangerous to allow the mind to hold any thought which is destructive. Such thoughts must sooner or later seek release through physical action.

Through the principle of Auto-Suggestion—that is, thoughts held in the mind and concentrated upon—any thought will soon begin to crystallize into action.

If the principle of Auto-Suggestion were generally understood and taught in the public schools, it would change the whole moral and economic standards of the world inside of twenty years. Through this principle the human mind can rid itself of its destructive tendencies by constantly dwelling upon its constructive tendencies. The qualities of the human mind need the sunlight of nourishment and use to keep them alive. Throughout the universe there is a Law of Nourishment and Use which applies to everything that lives and grows. This law has decreed that every living thing which is neither nourished nor used must die, and this applies to the qualities of the human mind which we have mentioned.

The only way to develop any quality of the mind is to concentrate upon it, think about it and use it. Evil tendencies of the mind can be blotted out by starving them to death through disuse!

There is nothing that savors of occultism in the human mind. It functions in harmony with the physical and economic laws and principles. You do not need the assistance of any person on earth in the manipulation of your own mind so it will function as you want it to. Your mind is something which you can control, no matter what your situation in life may be, provided always that you exercise that right instead of permitting others to do so for you.

Learn something of the power of your mind. It will free you of the curse of fear and fill you with inspiration, courage and happiness.

Success comes to those who become success conscious.

HOW TO ATTRACT PEOPLE TO YOU THROUGH THE LAW OF RETALIATION

OCTOBER 1919

To achieve fame or accumulate a big fortune requires the cooperation of your fellowmen. Whatever position one holds and whatever fortune one acquires must, to be permanent, be by sufferance of one's fellowmen.

You could no more remain in a position of honor without the goodwill of the neighborhood than you could fly to the moon, and as for holding a big fortune without the consent of your fellowmen it would be impossible, not only to hold it, but to acquire it in the first place, except by inheritance.

The peaceful enjoyment of money or position surely depends upon the extent to which you attract people to you. It does not require the farsighted philosopher to see that a man who enjoys the goodwill of all with whom he comes in contact can have anything within the capability of the people with whom he associates.

The roadway, then, to fame and fortune, or either, leads straight through the hearts of one's fellowmen.

There may be other ways of gaining the goodwill of one's fellowmen except through the operation of the Law of Retaliation, but if there is, this writer has never discovered it.

Through the Law of Retaliation, you can induce people to send back to you that which you give to them. There is no guesswork about this—no element of chance—no uncertainty.

Let us see just how to go about harnessing this law so it will work for us instead of against us. To begin with, we need not tell you that the tendency of the human heart is to strike back, returning, stroke for stroke, every outside effort, whether of cooperation or of antagonism.

Antagonize a person and as surely as two and two are four, that person will retaliate in kind. Befriend a person or confer upon him some act of kindness and he will also reciprocate in kind.

Never mind the person who does not respond in accordance with this principle. He is merely the proverbial exception. By the law of averages the great majority of people will quite unconsciously respond.

The man who goes about with a chip on his shoulder finds a dozen people a day who take delight in knocking it off, a fact to which you can easily subscribe if you have ever tried going about with a chip on your shoulder. You need no proof that a man who carries a smile on his face and who always has a word of kindness for everyone he meets is universally liked, while the opposite type is just as generally disliked.

This Law of Retaliation is a powerful force which touches the whole universe, constantly attracting and repelling. You will find it in the heart of the acorn which falls to the ground, and, in response to the warmth of the sunlight, bursts fourth into a tiny sprig consisting of two small leaves which finally grow and attracts to itself the necessary elements to constitute a sturdy oak tree.

No one ever heard of an acorn attracting to it anything except the cells out of which an oak tree grows. No one ever saw a tree which was half oak and half poplar. The center of the acorn forms affinities only with those elements which constitute an oak tree.

Every thought which finds abode in the human brain attracts elements after its kind, whether of destruction or construction, kindness or unkindness. You can no more concentrate your mind on hatred and dislike and expect a crop of the opposite brand than you could expect an acorn to develop into a poplar tree. It simply is not in harmony with the Law of Retaliation.

Throughout the universe, everything in the form of matter gravitates to certain centers of attraction. People of similar intellect and tendencies are attracted to each other. The human mind forms affinities only with other minds which are harmonious and have similar tendencies; therefore, the class of person which you attract to you will depend upon the tendencies of your own mind. You control those tendencies and can direct them along any line you choose, attracting to you any sort of person you wish.

This is a law of Nature. It is an immutable law and it works whether we make conscious use of it or not.

QUIT QUARRELING WITH YOUR FELLOWMEN

OCTOBER 1919

*If you cannot agree with others, you can at least
refrain from quarreling with them.*

The time and energy which we spend in striking back at those who anger us would make us independently wealthy if this great force were directed toward constructive effort—to building instead of tearing down!

It is the belief of this writer that the average person spends three-fourths of his or her lifetime in useless, destructive effort.

There is but one real way to punish a person who has wronged you, and that is by returning good for evil. The hottest coals ever heaped upon a human being's head are acts of kindness in return for acts of cruelty.

Time spent in hatred is not only wasted, but it smothers the only worthwhile emotions of the human heart and renders a person useless for constructive work. Thoughts of hatred do not harm anyone except the person who indulges in them.

Whiskey and morphine are no more deleterious to the human body than are thoughts of hatred and anger. Lucky is the person who has grown to be big enough and wise enough to rise above intolerance, selfishness, greed and petty jealousies. These are the things which blot out the better impulses of the human soul and open the human heart to violence.

If anger ever profited a man anything this writer never heard of it. Great souls are usually housed in human beings who are slow at anger and who seldom try to destroy one of their fellowmen or defeat him in his undertakings.

The man or woman who can forgive and truly forget an injury by a fellowman is to be envied. Such souls rise to the heights of happiness which most mortals never enjoy.

How long, oh God, how long, will it be until the human race will learn to walk down the pathway of life, arm in arm, helping one another in a spirit of love, instead of trying to cut one another down? How long will it be until we will learn that life's richest blessings are bestowed upon the person who scorns to stoop to the vulgar attempt to destroy his fellowman?

Deliberately seek the company of people who influence you to think and act on building the life you desire.

A PERSONAL INVENTORY OF MY THIRTY-SIX YEARS OF EXPERIENCE

DECEMBER 1919

I have often heard the expression "If I had my life to live over, I would live it differently!"

Personally, I could not truthfully say that I would change anything that has happened in my life if I were living it over. Not that I have made no mistakes, for indeed it seems to me that I have made more mistakes than the average man makes, but out of these mistakes has come an awakening which has brought me real happiness and peace of mind and abundant opportunity to help others find this much-sought state of mind.

I am convinced, beyond room for doubt, that there is a great lesson in every failure and that so-called failure is absolutely necessary before worthwhile success can be attained.

I am convinced that a part of Nature's plan is to throw obstacles in a man's pathway, and that the greatest part of one's education comes, not from books or teachers, but from constantly striving to overcome these obstacles.

I believe that Nature lays down obstacles in a man's pathway, just as the trainer lays down rails and hurdles for a horse to jump over while being trained to "pace."

Today is my birthday!

I shall celebrate it by doing my best to set down, for the readers of the little brown covered messenger, some of the lessons which my failures have taught me.

Let us begin with my favorite hobby, namely, my belief that the only real happiness anyone ever experiences comes from helping others to find happiness.

It may be a mere coincidence that practically twenty-five of my thirty-six years were very unhappy years and that I began to find happiness the very day I commenced helping others find it, but I do not believe so. I believe this is more than a coincidence—I believe that it is in strict accordance with a law of the universe.

My experience has taught me that a man can no more sow a crop of grief and expect to reap a harvest of happiness than one could sow thistles and expect to reap a crop of wheat. Through many years of careful study and analysis I have learned conclusively that that which a man gives comes back to him increased many times, even down to the finest detail, whether a mere thought or an overt act.

From a material, economic standpoint, one of the greatest truths I have learned is that it pays handsomely to render more service and better service than one is paid to render, for just as surely as this is done it is but a question of time until one is paid for more than he actually does.

This one practice of throwing one's heart into every task, regardless of the remuneration, will go further toward the achievement of material, monetary success than any other one thing that I could mention.

But equally important is the habit of forgiving and forgetting the wrongs our fellowmen commit against us. The habit of "striking back" at those who anger us is a weakness which is bound to degrade and work to the detriment of all who practice it.

I am convinced that no lesson which my life's experience has taught me has been more costly than the one which I learned by eternally exacting my "pound of flesh" and feeling it my duty to resent every insult and every injustice.

I am thoroughly convinced that one of the greatest lessons a man can learn is that of self-control. One can never exercise any great amount of influence over others until he first learns to exercise control over himself. It seems to me of particular significance when I stop and consider that most of the world's great leaders were men who were slow to anger, and that the greatest of all the leaders down through the ages, who gave us the greatest philosophy the world has ever known, as it is laid down in the Golden Rule, was a man of tolerance and self-control.

I am convinced that it is a grievous mistake for any person to start out with the belief that upon his shoulders rests the burden of "reforming" the world or of changing the natural order of human conduct. I believe that Nature's own plans are working out quite rapidly enough without the interference of those who would presume to try to rush Nature or in any way divert her course. Such presumption leads only to argument, contention and ill feelings.

I have learned, to my own satisfaction at least, that a man who agitates and works up ill feeling between his fellowmen, for any cause whatsoever, serves no real constructive purpose in life. It pays to boost and construct instead of knocking and tearing down.

When I began the publication of this magazine, I commenced making use of this principle by devoting my time and editorial pages to that which is constructive and overlooking that which is destructive.

Nothing which I have ever undertaken in all of my thirty-six years has proved as successful or brought me as much real happiness as my work on this little magazine has done. Almost from the very day that the first edition went on the newsstands, success has crowned my efforts in greater abundance than I had ever hoped for. Not necessarily monetary success, but that higher, finer success which is manifested in the happiness which this magazine has helped others find.

I have found, from many years of experience, that it is a sign of weakness if a man permits himself to be influenced against one of his fellowmen on account of some remark made by an enemy or someone who is prejudiced. A man cannot truly claim to possess self-control or the ability to think clearly until he learns to form opinions of his fellowmen not from someone else's viewpoint, but from actual knowledge.

One of the most detrimental and destructive habits which I have had to overcome has been that of allowing myself to be influenced against a person by someone who was biased or prejudiced.

Another great mistake which I have learned by having made the same mistake over and over again is that it is a grievous mistake to criticize one's fellowmen, either with or without cause. I cannot recall any personal development which I have gained from my mistakes that has given me as much real satisfaction as that which I have experienced from the knowledge that I had, to some extent, learned to hold my tongue unless I could say something kind about my fellowmen.

I only learned to curb this natural human tendency of "picking one's enemies to pieces" after I began to understand the Law of Retaliation, through the operation of which a man is sure to reap that which he sows, either by word of mouth or by action. I am by no means master of this evil, but I have at least made a fair start toward conquering it.

I am convinced that every man should go through that unhappy, though valuable, experience of having been attacked by the newspapers and losing his fortune at least once in his lifetime, because it is when calamity overtakes a man that he learns who his real friends are. The friends stay by the ship while the "would-be's" make for cover.

I have learned, among other interesting bits of knowledge of human nature, that a man can be very accurately judged by the character of people whom he attracts to him. That old axiomatic phase "birds of a feather flock together" is sound philosophy.

Throughout the universe the Law of Attraction, as it might be called, continuously attracts to certain centers things of a like nature. A great detective once told me that this Law of Attraction was his chief guiding principle in hunting down criminals and those charged with breaking the law.

I have learned that the man who aspires to be a public servant must be prepared to sacrifice much and withstand abuse and criticism without losing faith in or respect for his fellowmen. It is rare indeed to find a man engaged in serving the public whose motives are not questioned by the very people whom his efforts benefit most.

The greatest servant the world has ever known not only gained the ill will of many of the people of his time—an ill will to which a great many of the present age have fallen heir—but he lost his life in the bargain. They nailed him to a cross, pierced his side with a spear and fiendishly tortured him by spitting in his face while his life slowly ebbed away. He set us a mighty fine example to follow in his last words, which were something like the following: "Forgive them, Father, for they know not what they do."

When I feel my blood rushing to my head in anger on account of the wrongs which my fellowmen do me, I find comfort in the fortitude and the patience with which the great Philosopher watched his tormentors as they slowly put him to death for no offense whatsoever except that of trying to help his fellowmen find happiness.

My experience has taught me that the man who accuses the world of not giving him a chance to succeed in his chosen work, instead of pointing the accusing finger at himself, seldom rises above mediocrity.

A "chance to succeed" is something which every man must go out and create for himself. Without a certain degree of combativeness, a person is not apt to accomplish very much in this world or acquire anything which other people covet very highly. Without combativeness, a man can easily inherit poverty, misery and failure, but if he is to get a grip on the opposite to these, he must be prepared to "contend" for his rights!

But note well that we said his "rights"! The only "rights" a man has are those which he creates for himself in return for service rendered, and it may not be a bad idea to remind ourselves that the nature of those "rights" will correspond exactly to the nature of the service rendered.

My experience has taught me that a child can be burdened with no heavier a load nor visited with a greater curse than that which accompanies the indiscriminate use of wealth. A close analysis of history will show that most of the great servants of the public and of humanity were people who arose from poverty.

In my opinion, a real test of a man is to give him unlimited wealth and see what he will do with it. Wealth which takes away the incentive to engage in constructive, useful work is a curse to those who so use it. It is not poverty that a man needs to watch—it is wealth and the attendant power which wealth creates, for good or for evil ends.

I consider it very fortunate that I was born in poverty, while in my more mature years I have associated rather closely with men of wealth; thus I have had a very fair demonstration of the effect of these two widely separated positions. I know I shall not need to watch myself so very closely as long as the need for life's ordinary necessities confronts me, but if I should gain great wealth it would be quite essential for me to see that this did not take away the desire to serve my fellowmen.

My experience has taught me that a normal person can accomplish anything possible of human accomplishment, through the aid of the human mind. The greatest thing which the human mind can do is to imagine! The so-called genius is merely a person who has created something definite in his mind, through imagination, and then transformed that picture into reality through bodily action.

All this, and a little more, have I learned during these past thirty-six years, but the greatest thing I have learned is that old, old truth of which the philosophers all down the ages have told us—that happiness is found, not in possession, but in useful service!

This is a truth which one can appreciate only after having discovered it for himself!

There may be many ways through which I could find greater happiness than that which I receive in return for the work which I devote to the editing of this little magazine, but frankly I have not discovered it, nor do I expect to.

The only thing I can think of which would bring me a greater measure of happiness than I already have would be a larger number of people to serve through the monthly messenger of good cheer and enthusiasm.

I believe one of the happiest moments of my life was experienced a few weeks ago, while I was making a small purchase in a store in Dallas, Texas. The young man who was waiting on me was a rather sociable, talkative, thinking type of young fellow. He told me all about what was going on in the store—a sort of "behind the curtains" visit, as it were—and wound up by telling me that his store manager had made all of his people very happy that day by promising them a subscription to *Hill's Golden Rule Magazine*, with the store's compliments. (No, he didn't know who I was.)

That interested me, naturally, so I asked him who this Napoleon Hill fellow was, about whom he had been talking. He looked at me with a quizzical expression on his face and replied: "You mean to say you never heard of Napoleon Hill?" I confessed that the name did sound rather familiar, but I asked the young man what it was that caused his store manager to give each of his employees a year's subscription to *Hill's Golden Rule*, and he said: "Because one month's issue of it has converted one of the grouchiest men we've got into one of the best fellows in this store, and my boss said if it would do that, he wanted all of us to read it."

It was not the appeal to my egotistical side which made me happy as I shook hands with the young man and told him who I was, but to that deeper emotional side which is always touched in every human being when he finds that his work is bringing happiness to others.

This is the sort of happiness which modifies the common human tendency toward selfishness and aids evolution in its work of separating the animal instincts from the human intuition in human beings.

I have always contended that a man should develop self-confidence and that he should be a good self-advertisement, and I am going to prove that I practice that which I preach on this subject by boldly asserting that if I had an audience as great as that which is served by *The Saturday Evening Post*, which I could serve monthly through this little magazine, I could accomplish more inside of the next five years toward influencing the masses to deal with each other on the Golden Rule basis than all the other newspapers and magazines combined have done in the last ten years.

"Whatsoever a man soweth that shall he also reap."

Yes, it came from the Bible, and it is sound philosophy which always works. And my many years of experience have proved conclusively that it does.

The first time the notion ever struck me to own and edit a magazine, some fifteen years ago, my idea was to jump on everything that was bad and pick to pieces all that I did not like. The gods of fate must have intervened to keep me from starting such an ill-advised enterprise at that time, because everything that I have learned in thirty-six years of experience fully corroborates the philosophy in the above quotation.

There would be no advantage to be gained
by sowing a field of wheat if the harvest
did not return more than was sown.

WHY SOME MEN SUCCEED

DECEMBER 1919

When defeat overtakes a man, the easiest
and the most logical thing to do is quit.
That's exactly what the majority of men do.

We have made an important discovery—a discovery which may help you, whoever you are, whatever may be your aim in life, to achieve success.

It is not the touch of genius, with which some men are supposed to be gifted, which brings success!

It is not good luck, influence nor wealth!

The real thing upon which most great fortunes were built—the thing which helps men and women rise to fame and high position in the world—is easily described:

It is simply the habit of completing everything one begins, first having learned what to begin and what not to begin.

Take inventory of yourself covering the past two years, let us say, and what do we discover?

The chances are about fifty to one that we will discover that you have had many ideas, started many plans, but completed none of them!

You have heard it stated in axiomatic phraseology ever since you were old enough to remember that "procrastination is the thief of time," but because it seemed like a preachment you paid no heed to it.

That axiom is literally true!

You cannot possibly succeed in any undertaking, whether it is large or small, important or otherwise, if you merely think of that which you would like to accomplish and then sit down and wait for the thing to materialize without patient, painstaking effort!

Nearly every business which stands out prominently above the common run of similar businesses represents concentration on a definite plan, or idea, from which there has been but little, if any, variance.

The United Cigar Stores' merchandising plan is built upon an idea, simple enough, but upon which concentrated effort has been directed.

The Piggly-Wiggly retail stores were built upon a definite plan, through the principle of concentration, the plan itself, the concept of "cafeteria-style" shopping, being simple and easy of application to other lines of business.

The Rexall Drug Stores were built upon a plan, through the aid of concentration.

The Ford automobile business is nothing more than concentration upon a simple plan, the plan being to give the public a small, serviceable car for as little money as possible, giving the buyer the advantage of quantity production. This plan has not been materially changed in the last twelve years.

The great Montgomery Ward & Company and Sears, Roebuck & Company mail order houses represent two of the largest merchandising enterprises in the world, both having been built upon the simple plan of giving the buyer the advantage of quantity buying and selling and the policy of "satisfying" the customer or giving him his money back.

Both of these great merchandising concerns stand out as mammoth monuments to the principle of sticking to a definite plan, through concentration.

There are other examples of great merchandising success which were built upon the same principle, by adopting a definite plan and then sticking to it to the end!

However, for every great success to which we can point as a result of this principle, we can find a thousand failures or near failures where no such plan has been adopted.

This writer was talking to a man a few hours before writing this editorial—a man who is a bright and, in many ways, a capable businessman, but he is not succeeding for the simple reason that he has too many ideas and follows the practice of discarding all of them before they have been fairly tested.

This writer offered him a suggestion which might have been valuable to him, but he replied immediately—"Oh, I've thought of that several times, and I started to try it out once, but it didn't work."

Note the words well: "I started to try it out once, but it didn't work."

Ah, there was where the weakness might have been discovered. He "started" to try it out.

Reader of the *Golden Rule*, mark these words: It is not the man who merely "starts" a thing who succeeds! It is the fellow who starts and who finishes in spite of obstacles!

Anybody can start a task. It takes the so-called genius to muster up enough courage, self-confidence and painstaking patience to finish that which he starts.

But this is not "genius"; it is nothing but persistence and good, common sense. The man who is accredited with being a genius usually is, as Edison has so often told us, nothing of the kind—he is merely a hard worker who finds a sound plan and then sticks to it.

Success rarely, if ever, comes all in a bunch or in a hurry. Worthwhile achievement usually represents long and patient service.

Remember the sturdy oak tree! It does not grow in a year, nor in two, nor even three years. It requires a score of years or more to produce a fair-sized oak tree. There are trees which will grow very large in a few years, but their wood is soft and porous and they are short-lived trees.

The man who decides to be a shoe salesman this year, then changes his mind and tries farming the next year, and then switches again to selling life insurance the third year is more than apt to be a failure at all three, whereas had he stuck to one of these for three years, he might have built a very fair success.

You see, I know a great deal about that which I am writing because I made this same mistake for almost fifteen years. I feel that I have a perfectly good right to warn you of an evil which may beset your pathway because I have suffered many defeats on account of that evil and, consequently, I have learned how to recognize it in you.

The first of January—the day for good resolutions—is nearing. Set aside that day for two purposes and you will be quite likely to profit by having read this editorial.

First: Adopt a Chief Aim for yourself, for the next year at least, and preferably for the next five years, and write out that aim word by word.

Second: Determine to make the first plank in the Chief Aim platform read something after this fashion: "During the ensuing year I will determine as nearly as possible those tasks which I shall have to perform from start to finish in order to succeed, and nothing under the sun shall divert my efforts from finishing every task which I begin."

Nearly every man has intelligence enough to create ideas in his mind, but the trouble with most men is that those ideas never find expression in Action!

The finest locomotive on earth is not worth a dollar, nor will it pull a single pound of weight, until the stored-up energy in the stream dome is released at the throttle!

You have energy in that head of yours—every normal human being has—but you are not releasing it at the throttle of Action! You are not applying it through the principle of concentration to the tasks which, if completed, would place you on the list of those who are regarded as successes.

Usually a man will release that flow of action which he has stored up in his head in connection with a task which he delights in performing. That is the reason why a man ought to engage in the work which he likes best.

There is a way of coaxing that wonderful mind of yours to give up its energy and pour it out into action through concentration upon some useful work. Keep on searching until you find the best possible way of releasing this energy. Find the work through which you can release this energy most readily and most willingly and you will be getting mighty near to work in which you will find success.

It has been this writer's privilege to interview many so-called great men—men who were regarded as "geniuses"—and as a means of encouragement to you I want to tell you frankly that I found nothing in them which you and I and all of the other "ordinary" fellows do not possess. They were exactly like us, with no more brains—sometimes with less—but what they had, which you and I also have but do not always use, was the ability to release the action which is stored up in their heads and keep it concentrated upon a task, great or small, until completed.

Do not expect to become adept at concentration the first time you try. Learn first to concentrate upon the little things you do—the sharpening of a pencil, the wrapping of a package, the addressing of a letter, and so forth.

The way to attain perfection in this wonderful art of finishing all that you start is to form the habit of doing this in connection with every task you perform, no matter how small. The first thing you know, this becomes a regular habit and you do it automatically, without effort.

Of what importance will this be to you? What a useless, silly question—but listen and we shall answer: It will mean the difference between failure and success, disappointment and happiness!

THE HAPPY MIDDLE GROUND

DECEMBER 1919

Until you have learned to be tolerant with those
who do not always agree with you, until you have cultivated
the habit of saying some kind word of those whom
you do not admire, until you have formed the habit
of looking for good instead of bad, you will
be neither successful nor happy.

The purpose of schooling and of education is to develop in a person a sense of proportions. When a man begins to lose his sense of proportion on any subject, or before he develops this sense, he is known as an "eccentric" or a person who is slightly "off"!

Strictly speaking, we suppose there is no such thing as a perfectly balanced mind, but this is the sort of a mind which evolution is undoubtedly aiming to develop.

The well-educated person is the person who has developed a well-rounded sense of proportions. To be really educated, a person must be somewhat of a philosopher—he must acquire the habit of studying causes by their effects, or, inversely, of studying effects by their causes.

When you commence to analyze, inquire into and ascertain the component elements of any problem or subject, you are beginning to develop a sense of proportion.

The well-balanced mind is an analytical, inquiring mind!

Intolerance is one of the most destructive qualities with which the human race is cursed. We have reason to believe that an analytical, inquiring mind is seldom, if ever, intolerant.

When a man renders judgment on any subject without having heard the evidence or examined all of the available facts, he surely could not be called an analytical man, nor could it be said of him that he had developed a fair sense of proportions.

Let us remember that there is a cause for every effect! If the effect of our efforts in life is not pleasing, we should remember that it is a good plan to analyze and inquire into the cause! If we are not succeeding, it is about a hundred-to-one bet that we may find the cause by stepping to a looking glass.

We do not control all causes which affect us in this world, but may it not be possible that we do control enough causes to change the effects we produce which are undesirable? May it not be possible that we can control enough causes to considerably change our attitude toward others and the attitude of others toward us?

When you write out that "Chief Aim" which you intend to put into use, let us suggest that one of the planks in your platform read something after this fashion:

"During the ensuing year, I will make a special effort to develop a fair sense of proportion by making it a habit to analyze, inquire into and examine the cause of all effects which in any way affect the object of my lifework, my peace of mind, or my material success."

SUCCESS!

FEBRUARY 1920

Face the facts squarely. Ask yourself definite
questions and demand direct replies.

We are writing on January 1, 1920. Throughout the world, men and women are wishing and praying for success during the coming year.

Most of us are asking for success without the usual hardships which come with it. We want success with as little effort as possible.

May it not be well to define success, as we understand it, and write out a description of it, as one of the items on our list of hoped-for achievements for the coming year?

We do not know what your definition of the term *success* is, but if we may impose our own definition on you, we would do so about as follows:

Success is the sum total of one's acts and thoughts which have, on account of their positive, constructive nature, brought happiness and good cheer to the majority of those with whom one will be thrown in contact the coming year.

If you cause other people to smile when you are near; if you carry with you that rich, vibrating, dynamic personality which causes people to be glad when you are present; if you speak and think of the beauties of life and persuade others to do the same; if you have eliminated cynicism, hatred, fear, and despondency from your own nature and filled their places with a wholesome love for all humanity, then you are bound to be a success!

Money is not evidence of success! It may be, in fact, evidence of failure, and will be if happiness and goodwill did not accompany it throughout the process through which it was accumulated.

This writer values more highly than all the wealth in the world the pleasure—the thrilling joy—the happiness and contentment which has come to him as a result of the opportunity which he has had during the past year to serve his fellowmen through the pages of this magazine.

Could any amount of money buy such pleasure? No! A thousand times, no! Pleasure comes from doing and not from acquiring! This is a lesson which some people seem never to learn, but it is a truth, nevertheless.

The roadway to that thing which we call success leads only in one direction, and that is straight through the great field of human service. Any road which leads in other directions cannot possibly reach success.

This writer intends to try to be happier this year than he was last, not by "acquiring" more worldly goods, although he could use these to advantage, but by serving more people through this magazine and by bringing greater happiness to the members of his immediate family and his personal friends.

If we cannot increase our measure of success in this manner, then we know not how to do so! By no means do we recommend that anyone give up the pursuit of money as one means of finding success and happiness, but we strongly recommend that no one depend entirely upon the power of money for success.

We have never had enough money to cause us to quit trying to render service, but some whom we know have had, and the result was not what we call success. It was disheartening to observe. When they stopped serving others, they lost hope, they lost interest, and they gave up the most important thing they had achieved, their own peace of mind.

FINANCIAL SUCCESS IS DANGEROUS

FEBRUARY 1920

Financial success brings power, and power is a dangerous thing to those who have not learned how to use it justly and wisely.

Great financial power has a decided tendency to develop intolerance and disregard for the rights of others.

When you begin to succeed financially, you will need to watch your step more closely than ever before.

Financial success too often smothers the finer impulses of the human heart and leads a person to the worship of the god of Mammon!

It is the exception and not the rule when a man who accumulates great financial power without having tasted liberally of the dregs of poverty uses that power wisely.

Real success cannot be measured in dollars! It is something which can be measured only by the quantity and the quality of service which one renders for the good of others.

If financial power takes away the desire to render useful service, then it may be properly interpreted as failure instead of success.

We do not know for sure, but we strongly suspect that the only real success is that which brings happiness to oneself and to others. We also suspect that the only sure means of attaining happiness is through some sort of useful service which helps others to find happiness. Financial power doesn't always do this.

Watch your step as you begin to accumulate more money than you need for your daily use. Take care that it does not blind your eyes to the one sure pathway to real success, happiness and peace of mind, which is the performance of useful services for the good of humanity.

Money is either a good or a bad influence. It all depends on the character of the person who possesses it.

ENTHUSIASM

FEBRUARY 1920

Enthusiasm is contagious, and the person who has it
under control is generally welcome in any group of people.

Enthusiasm is one of the most desirable of qualities! It attracts people to you and causes them to cooperate with you.

Enthusiasm is the spark which touches off that dormant power which is housed in your brain and puts it into action.

Enthusiasm is a sure antidote for laziness and procrastination; it is the main spring which keeps your mental machinery in action.

Enthusiasm overcomes despondency and generates hope, self-confidence, and courage. Enthusiasm arouses your whole being and causes you to transform your dreams into reality! If you are not enthusiastic over your work, you do not love it; therefore, you are trying to perform work for which you are not fitted.

Enthusiasm is contagious! Unconsciously you pass it on to those with whom you come in contact and it arouses them to act and think as you do.

An enthusiastic person, when guided by a sense of justice toward others, is usually a great asset in any organization, business, family or community.

Are you a person of enthusiasm?

TWO ONE-LEGGED MEN!

FEBRUARY 1920

In the town of Wichita Falls, Texas, I saw a one-legged man sitting on the sidewalk begging for alms.

A few questions brought out the fact that he had a fair education. He said he was begging because no one would give him work. "The world is against me and I have lost confidence in myself," he said.

Ah, there was the rub!

"I have lost confidence in myself."

Across the hall from my office is another one-legged man. I have known him for several years and I know that his schooling was slight. He has less training than the one-legged beggar.

But he is earning a thousand dollars a month. As Sales Manager of a manufacturing concern, he is directing the efforts of fifty men.

The beggar displayed the stump of his amputated leg as evidence that he needed alms. The other one-legged man covered up the stump of his lost leg so it would not attract attention.

The difference between the two men exists merely in viewpoint. One believes in himself and the other does not! The one who believes in himself could give up the other leg and both of his arms and still earn a thousand dollars a month. He could even give up both eyes, to boot, and still earn the money.

The world never defeats you until you defeat yourself. Milo C. Jones, of "Little Pig Sausage" fame, became a wealthy man from the sausage business after paralysis had taken away the use of nearly every muscle in his body. He couldn't turn over in bed without aid.

As long as you have faith in yourself and that wonderful mind of yours continues to function properly, you cannot be defeated in any legitimate undertaking. This statement is made without qualifications because it is true.

If you have a strong belief in what you are doing
and what you want to do, no adversity
is too difficult to overcome.

SELF-CONTROL

MARCH 1920

You can never become a great leader nor a person of influence in the cause of justice until you have developed great self-control.

Before you can be of great service to your fellowmen in any capacity you must master the common human tendency of anger, intolerance, and cynicism.

When you permit another person to make you angry, you are allowing that person to dominate you and drag you down to his level.

To develop self-control, you must make liberal and systematic use of the Golden Rule philosophy; you must acquire the habit of forgiving those who annoy and arouse you to anger.

Intolerance and selfishness make very poor bedfellows for self-control. These qualities make impossible the development of self-control.

The first thing the shrewd lawyer usually does when he starts to cross-examine a witness is to make the witness angry and thereby cause him to lose his self-control.

Anger is a state of insanity!

The well-balanced person is a person who is slow to anger and who always remains cool and calculating in his procedure. He remains calm and deliberate under all conditions.

Such a person can succeed in all legitimate undertakings! To master conditions, you must first master self! A person who exercises great self-control never slanders his neighbor. His tendency is to build up and not to tear down. Are you a person of self-control? If not, why do you not develop this great virtue?

RETALIATION

MARCH 1920

Success requires no explanations. Failure permits no alibis.

Like attracts like!

We see concrete evidence of this principle in every act and in every thought. Failure attracts failure, while success attracts success.

All down the ages, the philosophers, seers and prophets have told us of this law, but generally they have stated it in axiomatic terms which have seemed to us abstract and more or less in the nature of preachments.

If you want evidence that such a law really exists, criticize the preacher, the lawyer, the doctor, or the average layman and see whether he retaliates in kind or not.

Reverse the rule and speak in complimentary terms of one of these and see whether or not he responds in kind.

The tendency of the human mind is to "strike back." If you present your neighbor with a gift, he sends something in return; but if you slander your neighbor, he likewise slanders you in return.

If you hate the world, it hates you in return; but if you have learned to forgive and forget, your shortcomings will likewise be forgiven and forgotten.

"Whatsoever a man soweth, that shall he also reap."

If you wish to enjoy an unusual experience, send Christmas or birthday cards to all whom you dislike and whom you believe dislike you. Write some appropriate little message on each and dismiss all feeling of hatred which you have been harboring in your heart. Your action will be more than likely to convert your enemies into friends. You can induce people to act toward you as you wish them to by taking the lead, through the Law of Retaliation, and setting whatever example you wish them to follow. Try it! You'll never regret it.

ALIBI BUILDERS

APRIL 1920

One of the commonest of mistakes is that of finding an excuse or creating an alibi to explain the reason why we do not succeed.

This would be just the thing if it were not for the universal tendency to look every place except the right place for this excuse, which is the nearest looking glass.

Last year we had a man on our staff who always had the very best sort of reason for all that he did not accomplish.

He is not with us any longer! He gravitated on and out, joining the ranks of those untold millions which constitute 98 percent of the people of the world—the fellows who do not succeed.

If you asked him his side of the story, he would undoubtedly say there was nothing wrong with him; his trouble was that this magazine did not appreciate a fine fellow like him!

It takes a courageous man—a big man—an honest man—to look himself squarely in the face and say, "I am looking at the fellow who is standing between me and success—get out of the way so I can pass!" We haven't found many such persons, but wherever you find one you find a man who is doing worthwhile things, who is serving the world constructively and usefully.

It may give one a certain amount of satisfaction to charge others with his failure and with his poor lot in life, but this practice surely does not tend to improve one's station in life.

I ought to know, for I must confess that I have tried it just enough in my time to find out that it will not work!

I have in mind a very dear friend who works rather closely to me in the business world. I know him well enough to feel privileged to tell him just what I believe to be his chief handicaps, but up to the present the only results have been to hear him find a fault with me to match every one that I find in him.

And, perhaps he is right; perhaps I have more faults than he has, but the big point that I want the readers of these lines to get, remember and make use of is this: It makes no difference what faults this chap may find in me or in others, he will sink or swim, rise or fall, on his own merits, and unless he quits building alibis and goes to building character by looking himself squarely in the face, he will wind up just where all alibi builders end—in the scrap heap of failure!

We all love to be flattered, but none of us loves to hear the truth about our faults. Some flattery is a mighty fine thing. It urges us on to undertake more, but too much of it causes us to lapse into inertia.

If I had no enemies, it would be necessary for me to go out and punch my finger in someone's eyes and make a few, because I need someone to keep me on the jump; to keep me from being self-satisfied; to keep me on the defensive in one way or another. When I am defending myself, I am growing stronger, developing my strategic ability and keeping in fighting trim so that when I need to fight, I will know how to fight.

It will do you no good to spend time looking for faults in those whom you do not like, or in those who have been courageous enough to point out yours to you, or in those who have outdistanced you in the game of life and are succeeding while you have failed. They have faults, make no mistake about that, but the time you spend proving that they have faults is time wasted, because you can make no use of this proof after you get it. Better by far that you spend this time checking up on yourself to find out why you have not succeeded and how you may eliminate those faults which have been pointed out to you.

You will not enjoy this as much as you would enjoy the applause of indulgent, admiring friends, but it will do you a lot more good in the long run in helping find success and peace of mind.

THE WAY OF SUCCESS IS THE WAY OF STRUGGLE!

APRIL 1920

Strength and growth come only through
continuous effort and struggle.

I come back, once more, to claim your attention for a few minutes on a subject which has made a tremendous impression on my mind during the past few years.

The conclusions which I have reached have been the only ones that a man with an open mind could have reached. I have seen so much evidence of the soundness of the principle which I shall pass on to you that I can recommend it to you as being worthy of your earnest consideration.

If a brick could talk, no doubt it would complain when it is placed in a red-hot kiln and burned for hours; yet that process is necessary in order to give the brick lasting qualities that will withstand the onslaught of the elements.

The prize fighter must take a great deal of punishment before he is ready to step into the ring and meet an adversary, yet if he fails to take that punishment and prepare for the final battle, he is sure to pay with defeat.

My little son has just staggered into my study with wobbly legs and with tears in his eyes. He just received a hard fall a moment ago while trying to balance himself on those little legs. He is learning to walk. He would never walk if he did not get many a fall and keep on trying.

The eagle builds her nest far above the tops of the trees, on some rugged crag in the cliffs, where no depredating man nor animal can reach her young. But, after taking all this precaution to protect her young, she will subject them to another danger just as soon as she believes they are ready to learn to fly. She will take them out to the edge of the rocks, push them over and "make them fly." Of course, she is right there to take the plunge with them, and if they are too weak to fly, she will dart under them, catch them in her claws, take them back to the nest and wait another day or so, then take them out again. This is the only way young eagles would learn to fly—through struggle!

And, as time and experience begin to extend my vision into the silent workings of Nature, I cannot help seeing that there is a guiding hand which pushes us into struggle that we may emerge with more knowledge of the things which we need to know in life.

The Law of Compensation is relentless in its work of helping man rise higher and higher through struggle! An athlete becomes an athlete only by practice, training, and struggle, just as a man becomes a doer only by doing! Some men learn easily and quickly, while Nature finds it necessary to break the hearts of others before they will recognize her handwriting on the walls of Time.

Back in my earlier days, before I had learned to read very much that Nature had written for my eyes, I often wondered when, where and how I would find myself; how I would know when I had come to myself; how I would know when I had found my lifework!

I suspect that this has worried many another!

To all such persons I bring a message of assurance and hope. You may be sure that as long as failure, heartaches and adversities come your way, Nature is struggling with you, trying to swerve your course in life. She is trying to switch you off the sidetrack of failure onto the main line of success.

Read the above paragraph again!

When you are unhappy, unsuccessful, and in trouble, there is something wrong! These conditions of mind are Nature's guideposts which point out to you that you are struggling in the wrong direction.

Make no mistake about this. Nature always points the way, and you will know when you are traveling in the right direction, just as definitely as you know when you have placed your hand on a red-hot stove. If you are unhappy, do not overlook the fact that this is an unnatural state of mind—that you have a right to happiness—and it is a sure sign that there is something wrong in your life!

Who ascertains what this "something" is that is wrong?

You do! Only you can do so!

A few souls—and they are rare indeed—follow Nature's guiding hand easily and readily. The Great Struggle with these people is not so painful. They respond readily when Nature touches them on the elbow with a stroke of adversity; but the majority of us have to be severely punished before we begin to realize that we are being punished.

Nothing is gained without something being given in return!

You may have whatever you want in this life if you will pay the price in struggle, sacrifice and intelligent effort. To this extent, you can avail yourself of the power of the Law of Retaliation, a law through the application of which you get exactly that which you give!

Stop worrying and fretting over your troubles and adversities and thank the Creator that he wisely placed guideposts in your pathway to help you right yourself. The normal state of mind is happiness. Just as sure as the sun rises in the east and sets in the west, happiness will come to the person who has learned to change his course when he comes to the mileposts of failure, adversity and remorse.

Most of us have heard of a certain word called "conscience," but few of us, indeed, have learned that this thing is a Master Alchemist which can turn the dross and base metals of failure and adversity into the pure gold of success.

When adversity, failure and discouragement seem to stare you in the face most unmercifully, let me give you this formula through which you can defeat these: Change your attitude toward your fellowmen and devote your entire efforts to the task of helping others find happiness. In your struggle, which is the price you must pay Nature in return for her work in transforming you, you will find happiness yourself.

To get it you must first give it away!

Do not sneer at this simple, homely advice. It comes from one who has tried the formula, knows it works, and, therefore, has the right to speak with authority.

After you have found happiness; after you have mastered that thing which you call your "temper" and have learned how to look upon all of your fellowmen with tolerance and compassion; after you have learned to sit down and calmly and serenely take inventory of your past, you will see, as clearly as you can see the sun on a bright day, that Nature has made you struggle as the only means of helping you find your way out of the darkness.

You will know, then, that you have found yourself. You will know, also, that struggle has its purpose in this life. You will know that the Creator took you out to the edge of the cliffs and pushed you over, just as the mother eagle pushed her young ones over, so you could learn to fly!

You will be at peace with all mankind, then, because you will see that the struggle which you had to make, as a result of opposition by your fellowmen, was the training you needed to find your place in the world. You will also see that you and not your fellowmen were the cause of this struggle.

This probably is the finest editorial I ever wrote, yet I feel sure that only those who have known what it is to fail, who have seen success grow out of the worst sort of failure, will appreciate it for all it is worth!

The others will appreciate it further down the road, after they have met with adversity, failure and discouragement; after they have discovered, just as I have done, that struggle is Nature's way of training the wobbly baby legs of mankind to walk.

A BRIEF STORY OF THE HUMAN MIND

APRIL 1920

At birth the mind is a blank; a great storage room with nothing in it but space.

Through the five senses of seeing, hearing, tasting, smelling, and feeling, this great storehouse is filled.

The sense impressions which find their way into this storehouse before the age of twelve are apt to remain there throughout life, whether they are sound or unsound.

Ideals and beliefs which are planted in the young, plastic mind of a child are apt to become a part of that child and remain with it throughout life.

It is possible to so impressively inject an ideal into a child's mind that this ideal will guide the child in its ethical conduct throughout life. It is possible to so thoroughly build character in the child's mind, before the age of twelve or fourteen years, that it should be practically impossible for that child to disregard that character and go wrong in later life.

The mind resembles a great, fertile field in that it will produce a crop after the kind of seed sown in it, by which is meant that any idea placed in the mind and held there firmly will finally take root and grow, influencing the bodily action of the person after the nature of the idea. Also, just as wild weeds will spring up in fertile soil that is not tilled, so will destructive ideas find their way into the minds of those who have not planted constructive ideas.

The mind cannot remain idle. It is always striving to produce, and naturally enough, it works with the material which finds its way into the mind as a result of our environment, our contact with others, the sights we see and the sounds we hear.

One of the most powerful principles of the mind is that known as Auto-Suggestion, through the aid of which we can continuously plant an idea in our own mind and concentrate upon it until it actually becomes a part of us to such an extent that it will dominate our actions and direct the movement of our bodies.

Another characteristic of the human mind is the fact that it becomes a sort of magnet or lodestone which attracts to us other people who think, believe and act as we do. The human mind has a strong tendency to reach out and form affinities with other minds with which it is in harmony on one or more subjects.

Throughout the universe there is a law through the operation of which "like attracts like." This law is seen in operation quite readily in the manner in which one mind will attract to it other minds which harmonize with it.

If this is a true statement, and we know that it is, can you not see what a powerful force this law is, and can you not see what a tremendous aid it can be to you if you will cultivate and constructively use it?

The human mind seeks its level just as surely as water seeks its level, and it will not be content until it finds its level. We see this working out in the mind of the man of literary tastes and tendencies who seeks the companionship of similar minds; in the wealthy man, who seeks companionship of the wealthy, and the poor man, who seeks the company of the poor.

If it were not for this law, the human body never would mature, for the reason that the chemicals, food and nourishment would never be attracted and distributed to the proper places for growth and expansion.

If it were not for this law, the material out of which fingernails are built would be distributed to the roots of the hair, or to some other part of the body where it is not needed.

This law is as immutable as the law of gravitation which holds this earth on its course and keeps every planet of the universe in its proper place.

Analyze your friends. If you are not proud of them, it is no particular credit to yourself, because you are the magnet which has attracted them. The color and tendency of your mind is the attraction which has gathered around you other minds which harmonize with your own. If you do not like those who have been attracted to you, change the magnet which attracted them and pick up another set of friends.

A mighty fine way to magnetize your mind so it will attract to you the highest standard of human beings is to set up in your mind an ideal that is patterned after men whom you most admire.

The modus operandi through which this is done is very simple and very effective! You can even draw on the character of sundry other people for material out of which to build, in your mind, this ideal which is to become the magnet that will attract to you those who harmonize with it.

For example, take from the life of Washington those qualities which you most admired in him, from Lincoln those qualities which you most admired in him, from Jefferson those qualities which you most admired in him, from Emerson those qualities which you most admired in him, and so on down the line. Out of the composite of these qualities build an ideal—in other words, see yourself possessing all of these qualities, permitting no act or thought to pass which does not harmonize with this ideal—and the first thing you know you'll begin to resemble this ideal, and, more important still, you will commence to attract to you others who harmonize with this ideal, either in whole or in part.

This is no mere theory. This writer knows that the plan works, because—well, because of the only reason that anyone knows anything, for sure—he has tried it himself!

You place the material in your mind and the Great Unseen Alchemist works it into shape, building you a character and a personality which correspond exactly to the nature of the material that you supply.

You now know how to gather the material!

You know how to be exactly what you want to be, and this writer will assume full responsibility for the soundness of this principle. It will work so that you, or even the most inexperienced unbeliever, can see that it works in time, ranging all the way from a few hours to a few months, depending upon the extent to which you concentrate your mind upon the task and the extent to which you see clearly the picture of the ideal or the person you are building.

This is Auto-Suggestion of which we are writing!

It is the principle through which you can build yourself over or through which you can build yourself to order. Through this principle you can master discouragement, worry, fear, hatred, anger, lack of self-control and the remainder of that long string of negative qualities which stand between most people and the full, happy, joyous life which is their right and heritage. These qualities are the weeds which correspond to those which spring up in the fertile soil of the fields when those fields are not plowed, cultivated and tilled.

This is not a new brand of religion of which you are reading; it is not a fad; it is not the outburst of an unbalanced, fanatical mind. It is a sound, scientific fact which any professor of psychology will corroborate.

These are just a few of the more elementary principles of your mind, stated in words which we intend to be so simple that a schoolboy or girl can understand them. For a more detailed study of that wonderful machine you carry around in your head, go to the library or to some good bookstore and buy a few books on Applied Psychology.

The only thing about you or anyone else that is really worthwhile is the mind! These old bodies that we carry around with us do not amount to much. They are merely the tools through which the mind operates, anyway. They cannot move an inch until the mind directs them to do so. If you would understand yourself, first learn something about your mind, and when you have learned a great deal about your mind you will know a great deal about all minds, because they all work in exactly the same manner.

LABOR AS A BLESSING AND AS A CURSE

MAY 1920

This editorial shows what it is that makes labor a curse; also, how and when labor becomes a blessing. It shows what will take the "curse" out of the most common sort of labor. It brings a message of hope to all who bemoan their lot in the world and points the way to improvement in unsatisfactory working conditions.

—EDITOR

The subject to which I invite your attention touches the interests of every man, woman and child. It enters into the daily life of humanity. Labor constitutes the warp and woof of every industry and every human good. It is not merely a question of bread, or of dollars and cents. It has a wider and deeper meaning than more or less abundance of clothes or acres. It is the cornerstone of social, civil and religious progress. It is a question of how to employ our time, to use our strength, to exercise our thought, to direct our affections in the wisest way to supply our natural wants and to secure the means of comfort, happiness and the development of the human facilities. It is, therefore, a question that confronts the individual, the state and the church at every step and presses for solution. It involves every effort to lighten human burdens, to alleviate human suffering, and to secure the order, comfort, prosperity, and happiness of the people.

It is not my intention to speak of organizations for the protection and advancement of the interests of the laborer or of the bearing of national or state legislation upon the subject. They have their influence and use. I propose rather to speak of labor in its application to the individual, to what every man and woman can do, today, in the present circumstances, in every condition, to remove the curse from labor and gain its greatest and most enduring rewards. It is my purpose to point out some remedies for the hardships which we all suffer, and which we can apply to our work tomorrow and every day of our lives. No combination of men can prevent the greatest curse of labor, no legislation can avert its evils or secure its greatest good. Let us, then, try to discover what the evils are that we desire to remove, and then we may be able to discover their remedies.

Strictly speaking, labor is not a curse or an evil in any sense. It is a blessing, not merely in its reward of wages, but in itself. Even in its most trying forms, it is better than idleness. This is the testimony of history and of individual experience in all ages of the world and of the Lord Himself. It exists in the nature of the human mind and is organized in every part of the material body. Look at a man from his limbs, his muscles, his brain, his senses, his intellect, his affections. What was he endowed with this miraculous organism for? What was he made for? To be idle? To eat and drink and sleep like an animal? Was the hand, that miracle of mechanism and power, made merely to use a spoon and wear gloves? To be kept soft like a baby's? What was every organ in the body made for? Was it not for man's happiness? How is he to secure the intended good? By use, by action, by labor. There is no other possible way. Action is the law of life; it is the effect and sign of life; it is the means of gaining larger measure of life; it is the essential instrument of perfecting life.

The higher we rise in the scale of being, the more irrepressible the activity. Let us learn a lesson from nature. The stone is motionless. It cannot change its form or place. Would you like to be a stone? The plant, though unconscious and anchored to the earth, is alive and full of action, and grows into a multitude of useful and beautiful forms. Here is more life, more action, and greater use. But would this satisfy you? Would you like to be an apple tree or a lily, though it neither toils nor spins? The animal stands in a higher grade of life. It can see, hear, feel, move, and act in many ways impossible to the plant. But would it content you to be an oyster or an ox? As we rise to man, we find a distinct and higher class of faculties. His range of action is vastly enlarged. He has more tools to work with, more labor to perform, and he gains larger and richer rewards. Every step of ascent in the scale of being demands greater and more varied labor by which we obtain a higher good.

No living creature is exempt from work. The worm and the fish and the four-legged animal must labor. Action in some form is the condition of existence. The fowls of the air of swift wings are constantly searching for food, and often they must go supperless to bed. A wild animal which has no master and is free to go and come, the idea which many entertain of a happy life, must keep on the alert for its dinner or go without it.

If man had never sinned, he could have found his happiness only in useful occupation. Every muscle in his body, and every faculty of his mind, reveals that fact more clearly than words have the power to do. The necessity for labor is organized in our minds and in every fiber of our bodies. If we could be fed with every luxury without lifting a finger; if we could be clothed like the lilies and be housed like a prince, without labor, we would be incomplete, because all our faculties are not only created by use, but their existence cannot be maintained without it. Consequently, every one, whatever may be his condition in life, must work. If he is not compelled by the necessity of earning his bread, he is driven by a sterner necessity to labor for pleasure, for digestion, and even for existence. Labor viewed in itself is a law of Divine order. It has its origin in the Divine perfections; it is universal in its application; it is the means to every good. This is the positive and unchanging fact.

CHRISTIANS, REAL AND PSEUDO

MAY 1920

We've noticed in our time that there are two brands of Christians. One the real, the other pseudo!

The latter is intolerant, wants to rule with an iron hand, never forgives, seldom forgets injuries or wrongs, and condemns all who do not agree with them.

The former—the genuine brand—says to those who injure and wrong them: "Forgive them, Father, for they know not what they do."

We've noticed, too, that not all church members are real Christians. Also, that not all non-church members are heathens.

Which also reminds us that we have gone about as far on this subject as we care to go, considering the fact that the policy of this magazine is not to enter into controversies on the subject of politics and religion or to try to change the belief of any person on either of these much-mooted subjects.

Our aim in editing this magazine—and it is an aim which is ever before us—is to help men and women learn that which we have learned; namely, that happiness on this earth can only be found by and through helping others find it. That success is within the reach of all who will develop and intelligently direct that God-given power called the human mind.

We bring you nothing through these pages which you do not already have, but we find it necessary in thousands of cases to help people find out the nature of that which they already have and show them how to intelligently direct it for the benefit of themselves and their fellowmen, who are their co-tenants here on earth, as they tarry by the wayside.

You can be anything you want to be,
if only you believe with sufficient conviction
and act in accordance with your faith.

ANOTHER POOR LITTLE RICH BOY

MAY 1920

Tell me how you use your spare time and how
you spend your money, and I will tell you where
and what you will be in ten years.

We read, in our daily paper, the following news item:

POOR LITTLE RICH BOY CAN'T LIVE ON $7,500 A YEAR

NEW YORK—A poor little rich boy of 17, who needs a new
$4,600 automobile and an increase in his allowance from
$7,500 to $10,000 a year, laid his appeal before Surrogate
Judge Cohalan today through his mother, saying the ever
mounting cost of living makes his present allowance of $7,500
a year inadequate for a boy of his station in life.

$7,500 a year is inadequate "for a boy of his station!"

Poor little fellow! Poor ignorant mother who suckled him at her
breast, nursed him through the dangerous period of babyhood, yet
proposes now to tie a weight around his neck which may deprive him
of initiative, which comes from the necessity of preparation to render
useful service to the world.

No seventeen-year-old boy can possibly and safely make legitimate use of $7,500 a year! The boy who has such an amount available is practically sure to develop the notion that he was made of superior clay to that used in the little fellows who labor in the shop and factory eight or ten hours a day, at wages of only a few dollars, most of which must go to pay rent, buy food and help support a family.

A few wonderfully useful men have been born of rich parents. John D. Rockefeller, Jr., would seem to be one of those whose inherited wealth did not spoil him to any noticeable extent.

With Harry Thaw it was different. Poor Harry was unfortunate in having an overindulgent mother and a father who provided too much money to back up that indulgence. It is more than likely that Harry Thaw would be a free, useful member of society today instead of having to be confined behind the walls of an insane asylum, a hopeless sufferer from dementia praecox, if stern necessity had moved him to work for a living when he was just entering manhood. Instead, this pampered young man murdered another, the talented architect Stanford White, in a jealous rage.

A course in business college, paid for by his own labor, and a job in a good business office, rendering service in return for his necessities, would have worked wonders with Harry Thaw.

We suspect that this "poor little boy" who must struggle along on $7,500 a year would be better off if his mother took about $500 of his next year's allowance and invested it in business college training for him.

This young fellow needs that subtle something which comes from the mixing and mingling with the sons and daughters of men who had the sound judgment to see that the best thing they could do for their children was to send them to business college and prepare them to render useful service.

Even one year of such wholesome training and mixing with young men and young women whose chief object, for the time being, is to prepare themselves to work, would work wonders in this little boy. We recommend this to his parents as being more beneficial to their son, in the long run, than the extra allowance would be, if granted.

If you doubt the wisdom of our recommendation, suppose you turn back the pages of history and study the really great men of the past: Socrates, Emerson, Aristotle, Epictetus, Shakespeare, Lincoln and a few of the others. Is it not worthy of consideration when we note that every one of these came up from the depths of poverty; that not one of them had any such allowance as $7,500 a year as a millstone around his neck to keep him from responding to the urgent call of stern necessity?

Take a look at the biographical records of some of our more modern successes, even those whose success is measured largely by the wealth they accumulated, and note how they, also, began at the bottom, without any yearly allowance other than that which they earned by the sweat of the brow. Take Carnegie, for instance, or Rockefeller Sr., James J. Hill or Henry C. Frick. Every one of these began as poor boys.

They rendered service because, at first, they had to render service! Out of necessity grew the habit of rendering service. Had not this force of necessity, sometimes called kind and sometimes unkind, followed at their heels, there is no telling how little these men might have accomplished.

Lincoln could easily have ended as Harry Thaw will end—in a grave unmarked by any constructive effort—had Lincoln been cursed with Harry Thaw's inheritance during his boyhood, while his character was being formed.

If you must give your boy money, wait at least until he has had a chance to develop that wholesome character which grows out of a love for delivering service. Wait until he grows up a bit and has developed some of those desirable characteristics which have marked the personality of the successful men who worked their way to the top from a humble beginning.

The money will keep. Lay it away in a bank and let it draw interest. Give the boy time to develop ability and intelligence with which to properly handle the money and then he may take his place in the pages of history alongside those to whom we point as successful and happy.

FOUR

"THINK AND GROW RICH WITH NAPOLEON HILL" RADIO PROGRAM

FEATURING HOWARD RAY AND NAPOLEON HILL

H. RAY: This radio broadcast will bring you in person the eminent success counselor, Napoleon Hill, author of the fabulous success book *Think and Grow Rich*. This is the book which has just been accorded fourth place among the books that have changed the lives of successful men and women all over America. In a national survey, reported in detail in the February 1948 issue of *Coronet* magazine, Napoleon Hill's book *Think and Grow Rich* was in fourth place in the minds of successful young men and women. You will discover why *Think and Grow Rich* was accorded this high place in the minds of successful men and women when you read it and when you learn to use the simple but brilliant rules for success contained within its covers. Ladies and gentlemen, meet the man who believes every person is entitled to success, Napoleon Hill. How do you do, Dr. Hill?

N. HILL: Fine. Thank you, Mr. Ray. It is a pleasure to be here and to talk to our new radio friends for a few minutes about their success.

H. RAY: Dr. Hill, in this interesting survey conducted by *Coronet* magazine and reported in the February issue, page 103, the successful people interviewed were asked one question that seems to me to be most interesting.

N. HILL: What was that, Mr. Ray?

H. RAY: They were asked, "What single ability is most essential to success?"

N. HILL: What single ability is most essential to success?

H. RAY: With emphasis on the word *ability*. In your rules for success, you show the principles of success which must be observed by the person in search of success, but our discussion today will be on the subject of ability—and of course, anyone's ability is improved by practice. So, I believe we have a very interesting talk ahead of us, Dr. Hill.

N. HILL: Yes, I'm sure we do.

H. RAY: All right. What single ability is most essential to success? Is it the ability to stay on the job day after day, and year after year, Dr. Hill?

N. HILL: The world is full of people who have been tied down to jobs all their lives, drudging along like automatic machines. But success seems to pass them by. I know a man who has worked as a clerk in a store for forty-two years. He started as delivery boy when he was just out of school, then he was promoted to part-time clerk, then later he was made a full-time clerk. He goes to work at the same time every day, goes to lunch at the same time and quits at the same time each evening. He's fairly pleasant to the customers and doesn't enter into much conversation with them, except for a few instances.

He's had a few raises—just enough to enable him to keep his bills paid and a few dollars left over, some of which he saves for the rainy day which is sure to come. If ability to stay on the job were the determining factor—if ability to stay on the job were the single ability most essential to success—then this man would be a brilliant success.

So you can see that this is not the answer, and we'll have to look farther.

H. RAY: Of course, it might be that these successful men and women mentioned by *Coronet* might have made a mistake in their conclusion as to what single ability was most essential to success, do you suppose, Dr. Hill?

N. HILL: No, I believe they hit the nail right on the head. I think they were exactly right in assuming that this one ability is most essential.

H. RAY: Well, I just wanted to be doubly sure that we weren't searching for an elusive answer that wouldn't be the answer at all when we did finally discover it.

N. HILL: No, I am sure we can continue our search in complete confidence that when the answer is finally found, it will be the right one.

H. RAY: Is the answer to be found in your book *Think and Grow Rich*, Dr. Hill?

N. HILL: Yes, indeed. It is to be found on many pages of *Think and Grow Rich*.

H. RAY: Well, that simplifies matters a great deal. All we have to do is to take a quick look at this book and we'll discover what ability is most essential to success.

N. HILL: Well, it won't be quite that simple, I guess, but if you take a real careful look, you can find the answer on many pages.

H. RAY: Well, here on page 39, in chapter 2, you were recounting the story of Edwin C. Barnes and his desire to become the partner of Thomas A. Edison. You said that Barnes burned all bridges behind him. When he went to Orange, New Jersey, he did not say to himself, "I will try to induce Edison to give me a job of some sort." He said, "I will see Edison and put him on notice that I have come to go into business with him."

Now from that remark I guess that Desire is the ability that is most essential to success. Is that correct?

N. HILL: Desire is a fundamental of success. Desire can be described as definiteness of purpose—knowing what you want. It is a vital factor, an important part of success, but it is not the ability for which we are searching at this time.

H. RAY: Well, I guess I can turn over a few pages then. I'll move over to page 71 in *Think and Grow Rich*. I'll bet I've found the most essential ability which those people who become successes must possess. Yes, I'll bet this is it—Faith.

On page 71 of the chapter on Faith, you say that "Faith is the eternal elixir which gives life, power and action to the impulses of thought." And you say that "Faith is the starting point of all accumulation of riches."

Certainly, if there is one ability that enables men to succeed, it must be the ability to have Faith in what they're doing. How about that, Dr. Hill? Am I right?

N. HILL: Well, Faith is a peculiar trait, but it is not an ability, for everyone has the same amount of Faith, strangely enough. The only difference in people is that one man will have Faith that he can accomplish a certain thing and the next man will have Faith that he can NOT accomplish what he is trying to do. Faith is directed either in your favor or against you, and you'd be surprised how many people direct their own Faith against themselves. More people have Faith in failure and sickness and unhappiness than in success and health and happiness.

So Faith is not an ability; it is a natural trait. And we either take full advantage of our Faith or we fail to take advantage. In many instances, we actually turn our Faith against ourselves and our own effort by believing in circumstances we do not want. No, Faith is not an ability. What we are searching for is the answer to what ability is most essential to success.

The dictionary says *ability* is "the power to perform." Sort of reminds me of the story of the settler who was considering the possibility of homesteading a farm in the early days. As I recall, this man asked an attorney friend about the law. Said the lawyer, "I don't know the exact text of the law, but I can give you the drift of it."

H. RAY: Yes, I remember that story. The lawyer said the general idea was that the government was willing to bet you 160 acres of land against $14 that you couldn't live on the land for five years without starving to death!

N. HILL: That would take a lot of ability, I guess, and so we are searching for the one ability that is most essential to success.

H. RAY: Maybe we've found it, Dr. Hill. Maybe it's sticktoitiveness, the ability to stay with a situation until you accomplish your purpose?

N. HILL: No, that's not it.

H. RAY: Well, I guess we had better move on to the next chapter in your book *Think and Grow Rich*. Maybe we can find it there. Chapter 4 may be the clue we've been looking for. Perhaps the answer is Auto-Suggestion, or self-hypnosis.

N. HILL: No, guess again.

H. RAY: How about the next chapter, "Specialized Knowledge"? Is that the ability most essential to success?

N. HILL: No, Specialized Knowledge will aid one greatly in attaining success all right, but it is not the one ability most essential to success, I can assure you.

As a matter of fact, the specialist may be entirely lacking in this essential. He may be a success in spite of lacking this one important thing we are searching for.

H. RAY: Chapter 6 in *Think and Grow Rich* is titled "Imagination." Maybe that is the thing we've been looking for!

N. HILL: At least, we're getting closer all the time. Anybody with Imagination will be able to discover and use this essential to better advantage than one without Imagination, I am sure.

H. RAY: Well, then how about chapter 7, "Organized Planning"? Will that help any in our search?

N. HILL: Yes, very much. A person with Imagination who does Organized Planning will, of necessity, recognize this ability which is so essential to success.

H. RAY: But in themselves, these two elements are not the ability for which we are searching?

N. HILL: No, they are not.

H. RAY: Then I guess we'll have to break down and ask you to name the one ability which is most essential to success. For every person certainly wants to know what that is, so he too may start using it as effectively as he knows how—as effectively as he can learn to use it. That is the reason so many people today are reading success books.

Now we have arrived at the point where we give up, Dr. Hill. Will you tell us the one ability which above all is essential to success?

N. HILL: Well, it's really quite simple. Since all success is predicated upon contact with other people, it's easy to see that the ability to get along with other people is the most essential to success.

H. RAY: Dr. Hill, do you mean that we can't pop off and tell people what we think about them?

N. HILL: The ability to get along with other people is the most essential of all success traits.

H. RAY: You mean I can't bawl out people who work for me?

N. HILL: The ability to get along with other people is the most essential of all success traits.

H. RAY: Can't I tell a customer what I think of him when I resent what he says about my merchandise?

N. HILL: The ability to get along with other people is the most essential of all success traits.

H. RAY: Can't I…oh, all right, I give up. But do you mean this always applies to everybody, Dr. Hill?

N. HILL: I am sure that this is the key to success.

H. RAY: Then you think the successful young men and women who were polled by *Coronet* correctly diagnosed this thing called success?

N. HILL: I most certainly do.

H. RAY: And that the most essential success trait really is the ability to get along with other people?

N. HILL: Of course, because all success is predicated upon our contact with other people. Other people are necessary in any calling in which we engage. There is no such thing as success for the man who is absolutely isolated from others, if that is ever possible.

H. RAY: Success, says Napoleon Hill, is by appointment only. And as we have pointed out in this discussion, the ability to get along with people is the most essential of all traits.

And does Napoleon Hill teach you how to get along with other people? Well, let's ask him.

Dr. Hill, in your philosophy of success, you include seventeen fundamentals. How many of those seventeen fundamentals deal directly with the subject of getting along with other people?

N. HILL: Five of these principles deal directly with that subject.

H. RAY: Then this subject of getting along with people is not new to you, is it?

N. HILL: Hardly. It is the one factor which I recognized at the very beginning of my research on this fascinating subject.

H. RAY: What five of your success principles deal with getting along with others?

N. HILL: The first one is the Master Mind principle.

H. RAY: For those who do not understand the meaning of the Master Mind, will you give us an easy-to-understand definition, please?

N. HILL: The Master Mind is a condition which exists when two or more minds work in perfect harmony toward a definite end.

H. RAY: That's a bull's-eye if there ever was one. Two or more minds working together in perfect harmony—is that getting along with other people? It had better be!

And the second of your success principles, Dr. Hill, which is on the subject of getting along with others?

N. HILL: An Attractive Personality.

H. RAY: And ladies and gentlemen, when you study the thirty factors of an Attractive Personality as taught by Napoleon Hill, you will know that he believes the most important ability of the successful person is his ability to get along with other people. Otherwise why would he even bother with such a subject as an Attractive Personality in a success philosophy?

And your next principle of success which deals with the ability to get along with other people, Dr. Hill?

N. HILL: Going the Extra Mile—that is, doing more and better work than you are paid to do, doing it all the time, and doing it in a positive, pleasing mental attitude.

H. RAY: Did somebody say something about getting along with other people? Where is there a better formula in all the world for getting along with those whom you contact? Can you imagine a better rule, regardless of whether you are an employee or an employer? Going the Extra Mile.

N. HILL: Yes, rendering more and better service than you are paid to render, doing it all the time and in a positive, pleasing mental attitude—try it and see if it contributes to your efforts to get along with others.

H. RAY: And this next principle in Napoleon Hill's philosophy of success fills the demands of every last person who has any religious leanings at all.

N. HILL: The Golden Rule, the rule that works every time regardless of your religious leanings.

H. RAY: What? The Golden Rule is not religion?

N. HILL: It may be part of religion, but it's not a part of any special doctrine or "ism," you may be sure of that. It's a part of the Universe. It's a law which was in effect when the world was created and will still be in effect after the Universe has disappeared. And it's a law that works in business and industry just as surely as it works anywhere else. When men get the idea that the Golden Rule is not working in their cases, they're due for a fall and a surprise. What you do to and for others you do to and for yourself.

H. RAY: And the thing which will surprise you who study Napoleon Hill's philosophy is the way he shows you HOW these principles work. He doesn't just say, "You should observe the Golden Rule because all good men observe it." Not at all. He says, "You may kid yourself, but you can't escape the immutable law of the Golden Rule. It works every minute you live, and the treatment you accord your fellowmen will return to you just as surely as night follows day. So if you want success to come back to you, you'd better start dishing it out now and keep on dishing it out as long as there's a breath of life in you."

I believe there's another principle in your success philosophy which has to do with getting along with other people, isn't there, Dr. Hill?

N. HILL: Yes, and that principle is Teamwork—friendly cooperation.

H. RAY: Is this principle anything like the Master Mind you mentioned a few minutes ago, Dr. Hill?

N. HILL: The Master Mind is the small inner circle of people who work with you in harmony, but Teamwork must include every single person with whom you are connected in a business way. Teamwork is cooperation for mutual benefits to all parties concerned. It is just plain common sense in the final analysis.

H. RAY: But it certainly is included in the ability to get along with other people.

N. HILL: Definitely. It is practically nothing else BUT getting along with other people.

H. RAY: So, you see, Napoleon Hill agrees with the opinion brought out in the survey conducted by *Coronet* magazine in the February issue. As a matter of fact, he has agreed with them for the past forty years, the length of time he has been creating this philosophy of individual success. Yes, it's true—the one ability most essential to success is the ability to get along with other people. You go even farther than that in your success philosophy, don't you, Dr. Hill?

N. HILL: Yes, I do. I go so far that I insist on my students taking the entire blame for everything that happens between them and other people.

H. RAY: Dr. Hill! Not everything!

N. HILL: Absolutely! In the final analysis, we are responsible for our own success or our own failure; therefore, we are responsible for every single thing that happens to us. And even if we are not, there is only one way to condition our minds for success—just one way to condition our thinking to the point where we take full and complete control of our minds—and that is to take the blame for everything that happens to us. There is no other way. Trying to put the blame for things that happen on other people is the way weaklings operate. I do not want my students to be weaklings. I want them to stand on their own feet. I want them to take complete charge of their own minds. I want them to demand success from the world and to attain success. Therefore, I insist that they take full responsibility for every last thing that occurs in their lives. Only in this way can we build minds that are strong, minds that are positive, minds that can stand success. For you must remember, it takes a strong mind to stand success. That's the real test of character. I have known many men who could stand failure fairly well, but when success came to them they were utterly unable to cope with the situation because they had not learned how to get along with other people. They had not learned the big lesson in success—that other people are partly responsible for one's success. Yes, there is no doubt that the ability to get along with others is the most essential element in success. For when you have learned how to get along with others, my friends, you are truly and finally at peace with yourself and at peace with the world.

H. RAY: Thank you, Dr. Napoleon Hill, for your fine discussion on the ability to get along with other people.

AFTERWORD

by Don Green

I hope you have enjoyed this book on the *Pathways to Peace of Mind*. I encourage you as well to read *Grow Rich with Peace of Mind*, Napoleon Hill's last book. It too will help you understand that a truly satisfying and rewarding life can be attained only when one finds peace of mind. Money may help you attain it, but it alone will not give you peace of mind. What will? Napoleon has identified a number of factors, traits, and principles, but the predominant one I have learned from his teachings is the act of helping others.

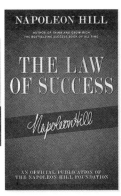